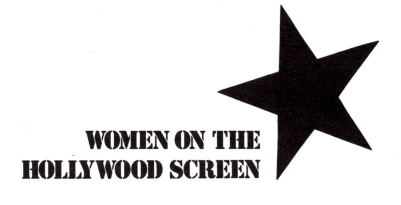

WOMEN ON THE
HOLLYWOOD SCREEN

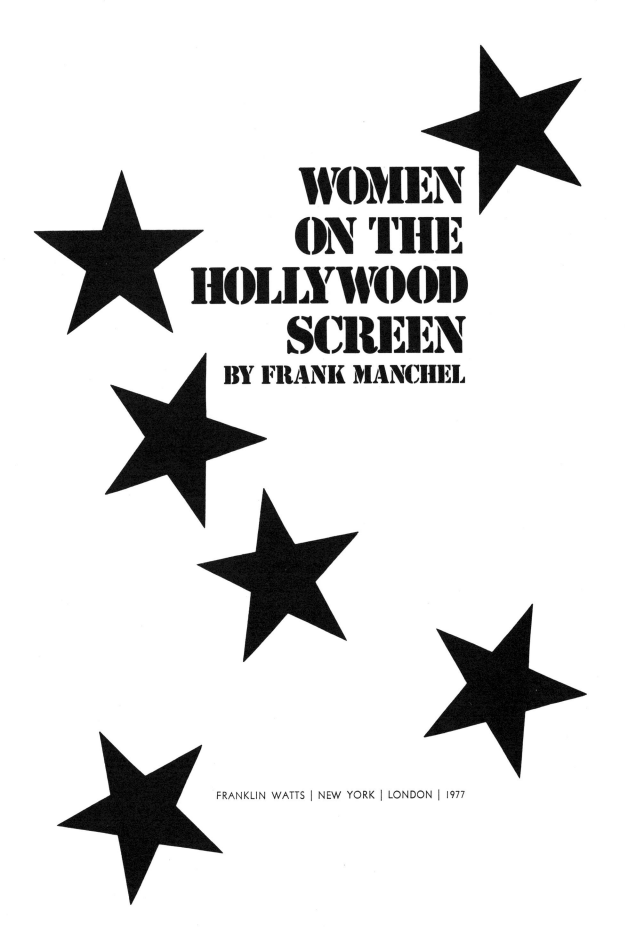

WOMEN ON THE HOLLYWOOD SCREEN

BY FRANK MANCHEL

FRANKLIN WATTS | NEW YORK | LONDON | 1977

To Barbara and Louis Wachtel:
more than blood, what binds us
together are love and respect

Library of Congress Cataloging in Publication Data

Manchel, Frank.
Women on the Hollywood screen.

Bibliography: p.
Includes index.
SUMMARY: Examines the history of film ac-
tresses and the characters they portray starting with
the early days of silent films.
1. Women in moving-pictures—Juvenile litera-
ture.   2. Moving-picture actors and actresses—
United States—Biography—Juvenile literature.   3.
Moving-pictures—United States—History—Juvenile
literature.   [1. Women in motion pictures.   2.
Motion picture actors and actresses.   3. Motion
pictures—History]   I. Title.
PN1995.9.W6M34   791.43'0909'352   76—56771
ISBN 0—531—00389—2

CONTENTS

Other books by
Frank Manchel

*Movies and
How They are Made*

*When Pictures
Began to Move*

*When Movies
Began to Speak*

Terrors of the Screen

Cameras West

*Film Study:
A Resource Guide*

*Yesterday's Clowns:
The Rise of Film Comedy*

*The Talking Clowns:
From Laurel and Hardy
to the Marx Brothers*

*An Album of Great
Science Fiction Films*

INTRODUCTION

What is a Hollywood woman?

Is she a loving wife like Julie Andrews in *The Sound of Music?* . . . a kookie friend like Liza Minnelli in *The Sterile Cuckoo?* . . . a bullying mother like Ann-Margret in *Tommy?* Is she a silent movie queen from the twenties? A love goddess from the thirties?

She is, clearly, all of these women and more. The Hollywood woman is an image of America's fantasies over the past seventy-odd years.

Not every generation has the same fantasies. Our desires are often based upon the everyday pressures of the age in which we live. Film makers, therefore, are always changing the image of women to keep up with the times.

The first movies, at the beginning of the twentieth century, showed the ties between society and woman. Although made purely for entertainment, silent movies were teachers. They taught their viewers, frequently immigrants, what the United States valued. People eager to move up the social ladder looked to movies to learn about social and sexual customs, as well as how to dress and spend their money.

The early films also educated our great-grandparents about a woman's place in society. Such actresses as Mary Pickford, the Gish sisters, and Mae Marsh showed the "right" way for young ladies to behave. They focused on loving their men and children. They were gentle, religious, and sensible. Most of all, these women never looked for happiness outside the home.

[1]

In *The Sound of Music* Julie Andrews gave one of the most popular performances in film history. She played Maria, a 1938 postulant who becomes a governess to seven children and falls in love with their widowed father, Baron von Trapp. Based on a true story, *The Sound of Music* won five Oscars in 1965, including best picture of the year.

Mary Pickford was the first great star of the movies. Known as "The Girl with the Curls," she is shown here in a scene from *Daddy Long Legs* (1919). The screenplay, written by Agnes Johnson, focused on Judy Abbott, an outcast who grows up in a cruel orphanage. In typical Pickford style, she leads a rebellion against the institution and proves that good always wins out in the end.

In contrast, there was Theda Bara, known as "the Vamp," who pointed out in her screen roles that sex was dangerous. It not only destroyed men but women as well.

After World War I America underwent sweeping changes. Various reform groups argued against liquor and for women's right to vote, and in 1917 and 1919 Congress passed the Eighteenth and Nineteenth Amendments.

It was a new era and a new woman appeared: the flapper. She smoked, bobbed her hair, wore short skirts, made up more than 20 percent of the working class, and had her own money to spend.

Hollywood, now the movie capital of the world, got in step with the times. Where once the movies had been a five-cent business, it now became a major industry. The men who ruled Hollywood built their empires on a star system; performers who appealed to mass audiences became famous celebrities. Aided by fan magazines, press agents, and publicity departments, the movie kings turned a strong personality into a star.

A twenties' flapper found her image in stars like Clara Bow and Colleen Moore. In films glorifying youth and love, these actresses catered to the new woman in society. The stress was on current ideas: health, beauty, body, and independence. These exciting women knew just how far to rebel against the old rules without getting into serious trouble.

Theda Bara showed audiences in the early 1900s everything Pickford was not. Stressing lust and danger, "the Vamp" made movies like *Cleopatra* (1918) to point out the dangers of uncontrolled sexual passion.

Clara Bow typified the flapper of the twenties. With her bobbed hair, painted lips, and accented eyes, she represented the newly liberated woman out for a good time with men. In the movie *It* (1927), Bow played Betty Lou, a working-class girl with sex appeal. Based on an idea by screenwriter Elinor Glyn, *It* set the glamour styles for millions of American women in the late twenties.

Not everyone, however, was happy with Hollywood's emphasis on sex and glamour. Reformers felt that the movies spent too much time showing the working-class woman in need of fun and freedom. They argued that the "new" ideas would cause dissatisfaction; they were dangerous and needed to be controlled. And so censorship found its way into the film business. Rules were drafted explaining what could not be shown in movies.

Then came the thirties and the Great Depression. Most people turned to the new talking pictures to escape the boredom and insecurity of their everyday lives.

By now Hollywood had used its successful star system to create powerful studio organizations. These fabulous studios operated like "factories." Everyone was a specialist. Each studio employed producers, directors, story writers, publicity men, and technicians to manufacture "products" starring the audience's most popular screen personalities. As audience tastes changed, new stars were "created." In short, like any other business, movies were made to satisfy the demands of the customers.

From musicals about chorus girls searching for rich husbands to gun molls swapping gags and insults with their tough boyfriends, the Hollywood woman proved to be the most popular factor in film. Metro-Goldwyn-Mayer (M-G-M) was the biggest studio, and except for such actors as Clark Gable and Spencer Tracy, females held the spotlight. Among the more famous stars were Joan Crawford, Jean Harlow, Myrna Loy, Greta Garbo, Norma Shearer, Judy Garland, Eleanor Powell, and Rosalind Russell. Paramount was the second biggest studio. It survived the thirties mainly because of its female stars Mae West and Marlene Dietrich. Third in order of importance was Warner Brothers. Among its most popular stars were Joan Blondell, Ruby Keeler, Barbara Stanwyck, Glenda Farrell, and Bette Davis. Twentieth Century-Fox owed its survival during the Depression years to Alice Faye, Janet Gaynor, and Shirley Temple.

Columbia was grateful for Jean Arthur; Radio-Keith-Orpheum (RKO) had Ginger Rogers; and Universal grew powerful with Deanna Durbin.

The star system, economic worries, and the censors forced the giant studios into "formula" film-making. Instead of making new and different types of movies, the studios relied on themes that had proved popular with audiences: love stories, gangster movies, westerns, and musicals. Each formula film acted as a test for a performer's audience appeal. Costumes, lighting, entrances, and exits were all designed to make the actress attractive to fans everywhere. Once a star proved her popularity, she became more important than the formula. It was her name, her face, her image that got all the publicity. Screenplays were made to fit her personality more than to fit the reality of film stories.

The effect was to create a dream world at the movies that ignored the setbacks that women faced in society. Instead of dealing with unemployment, for example, movies focused on wisecracking, fast-thinking, and beautiful women who more than held their own with men.

Understandably, those women who became superstars were as powerful offscreen as on. They used their popularity at the box office to get more money and better roles, and often they were able to break out of their formula films and create new images when audience tastes changed.

The coming of the forties forced film makers to turn their attention to more serious images of women. With America's entrance into World War II, and with most men in the armed forces, women became a larger portion of the work force. Doing "man's work" produced new fantasies for females. Patriotism became more important than fashions. Also, husbands, brothers, fathers, and sons overseas needed assurances that their loved ones back home were faithful and secure.

In keeping with the national spirit, the Hollywood woman adjusted the old formulas. Her roles narrowed down to a

Jean Harlow has often been compared to Marilyn Monroe. As the sex queen of the Depression years, Harlow dared men to look at her charms and not lose their senses. She mixed comedy with love and helped bring in the Motion Picture Code and its strict rules on sex in the movies.

few characters. She could be like Greer Garson in *Mrs. Miniver*, self-sacrificing and dedicated to her family, or like Rita Hayworth in *Gilda*, dangerous and destructive. She could even be like Betty Grable in *Coney Island*, beautiful to look at but always true to her one love.

By the time the fifties arrived, Hollywood was entering the most difficult stage of its short life. Part of the problem was the federal government. Congress was investigating alleged communist activities in the film industry. The Justice Department had forced the studios to give up their vast movie theater chains. The problem was accentuated by the rise of television, suburban living, and foreign films— new diversions diminished the large movie audiences that Hollywood had come to depend upon since the twenties. Another aspect of the dilemma was the return of men to their old jobs after the war, which forced many women once more to return to a traditional role in society.

Thus a frightened, confused, and desperate Hollywood tried to save itself by returning to the simple formulas so popular in the early days of film. Just as in the time of Pickford, the men who ran the industry suggested that there were only two ways for a female to behave. She could be the nice girl in search of a husband like Debbie Reynolds, Doris Day, Grace Kelly, and Audrey Hepburn. Or she could be the sex symbol out for a fling and headed

The reigning sex goddess of film during the forties was Rita Hayworth. Known as "The Intellectual Glamour Girl," she combined physical charm with brains. Glenn Ford, in this publicity shot from *Gilda* (1946), expressed what men felt for this desirable woman.

for trouble like Marilyn Monroe, Jane Russell, and Ava Gardner.

For a while, the changing situation in American movies during the sixties put an end to the old business formulas. Films were made and paid for by independent producers. The big studios took part only in the distribution of the films to the movie theaters. This new arrangement gave more freedom to the film makers in what could be shown and said.

Many of these independent film makers showed American society as corrupt and violent. They also presented the social revolution taking place as a result of the "pill," the widespread use of drugs, interracial marriages, the Vietnam war, and the civil-rights movement. The innocent heroines of the fifties were replaced by stories about single, sex-conscious, independent women. Among the most appealing of the new actresses were Shirley MacLaine, Julie Christie, Jane Fonda, Faye Dunaway, and Lee Remick.

Their films contained the mood of the sixties. From *The Apartment* (1960) to *They Shoot Horses, Don't They?* (1969), women were deglamorized. They were shown as unhappy people living in a sick society. The stress on the character's emotional problems led some viewers to think female roles were becoming more realistic. Romance and love had been replaced by sexual problems and violent life-

Marilyn Monroe was the supreme love goddess in the fifties. Fascinating both men and women with her sexual appeal and insecurity, she tried but never became a serious actress. This skirt-blowing scene in *The Seven Year Itch* (1955), was typical of her roles in film.

In Arthur Penn's sensational gangster film *Bonnie and Clyde* (1967), Faye Dunaway captured the violence of the sixties. Playful, innocent, and dangerous, she typified the independent film maker's renewed interest in neurotic women. Warren Beatty played Clyde.

styles. Yet a closer look at films revealed that the basic Hollywood formulas were still at work. Sex and violence were not new to movies. They had been there from the start. For that matter, neurotic women had also enjoyed a long popularity in films. What was new about the sixties was the importance given to sex, violence, and neuroticism.

But if independent film makers thought this was what audiences wanted, they were wrong. Profits went down, attendance dipped to a new low, and the audiences, confused by the sweeping changes that were taking place in society, sought comfort in those few formula musicals that reminded them of the old days. Thus, the most popular stars of the decade turned out to be newcomers Julie Andrews and Barbra Streisand.

The confusion over audience tastes almost destroyed the star system. Studios were putting more time and money into stories than into performers. As picture after picture failed at the box office, fewer movies were made. It just cost too much to produce lots of films. The result was that fewer roles were available to performers. Frightened producers searched for images of women that mass audiences could identify with. None was available. Dissension and confusion over society's values had divided the audience. Thus, as the decade progressed, the names and faces of the stars became less and less familiar. This, in turn, weakened a star's importance and power. If she couldn't prove her power at the box office, she couldn't gain any control over her film roles. Actresses Joanne Woodward and Cecily Tyson illustrated the dilemma of the stars. Despite their obvious talent, they couldn't find starring roles and had to content themselves with becoming major character actresses.

Adding to their problems was the fact that independent film makers lost faith in their own abilities to treat women in film and still make money. They turned their attention instead to male fantasies and ignored female roles. This gave rise to a series of "buddy" films, such as *Easy Rider*, *Midnight Cowboy*, *Butch Cassidy and the Sundance Kid*, *The Sting*, *The Last Detail*, and *Scarecrow*.

Today, American film makers are once again doing big business. Thanks to "blockbuster" movies like *The Poseidon Adventure* (1972) and fashionable nostalgia films like *American Graffiti* (1973), audiences by the millions are returning to movie theaters. Yet screen actresses still find themselves ignored. They get no credit for the industry's biggest profits since 1946. Film makers point to the current movie boom as proof that actresses do not appeal to an escape-minded public. The producers' formula is to keep women on the screen as little as possible.

The sharpest example of this practice was seen in the 1975 Academy Awards. Four out of five films nominated for Best Picture had women playing minor roles: *Dog Day Afternoon*, *Jaws*, *Barry Lyndon*, and *One Flew Over the Cuckoo's Nest*. The fifth film, *Nashville*, focused on a dozen different characters. When it came to the Best Actress category, the nominating board found few actresses even qualified to compete. In fact, Louise Fletcher, who won the Oscar for her role as the miserable Nurse Ratched in *One Flew Over the Cuckoo's Nest*, in better times would have been in the Supporting Actress category.

The question of who is responsible for the limited participation of women in American movies today has set off a debate within the film industry itself. Some actresses blame the male-dominated scriptwriters. "I'm sick and tired of seeing women portrayed as empty-headed," complains Marsha Mason, nominated for an Academy Award for her role as a promiscuous mother in *Cinderella Liberty* (1973). "They fail, lose, or die." Another actress with similar complaints is Susan Anspach, known best for her role as the confused wife in *Blume in Love* (1973). "In the scripts I get," she points out, "the woman is either a neurotic, a slut, a whore or somebody's daughter. Or else there are

Louise Fletcher won an Oscar for her role in *One Flew Over the Cuckoo's Nest* (1975). The character of Nurse Ratched was a supporting role and would not normally have been in the Best Actress category, except for the dearth of film heroines in the seventies. Jack Nicholson was the rebellious inmate (above left).

Ellen Burstyn stands today as one of the most forward-looking film actresses. Determined to change the place of women in the movies, she personally supervised the incidents and actions that won her an Oscar as the lonely widow in *Alice Doesn't Live Here Anymore* (1974).

the feminist films about women who hate men. There's never just a real person with real drives—sexual drives and life drives."

For a film maker like Robert Altman, men can't be blamed for the bad image of women in American movies. The director, whose films (*M*A*S*H*, *McCabe and Mrs. Miller*, *California Split*, and *Nashville*) often show neurotic and promiscuous women, comments, "Well, isn't that the way women are?" The producer of *The Godfather*, Al Ruddy, agrees: "It's only in recent times that a woman has functioned as anything beyond a mistress, show girl or nurse."

Clearly, the ways women are portrayed in film are signs of a long-term illness. There is no one cause and no one cure. Having more women in control would not automatically make conditions any better. Society has conditioned women to cherish the same values as men. The values endorsed in the popular novels of Jacqueline Susann are no less distorted than those of Harold Robbins.

At the core of the crisis is the fact that movies first and foremost are a business. Film makers base their efforts on what the public will pay to see. Because they feel audiences won't support movies starring women, major film makers refuse to produce them.

One way to change this is for more concerned women to become involved in the business end of films. Ellen Burstyn took this path following her success as a terrified mother of a child possessed by the devil in *The Exorcist* (1973). She demanded and got control over her future scripts and directors. Such a move made it possible for her to win an Academy Award in 1975 for her portrayal of a lonely widow in *Alice Doesn't Live Here Anymore* (1974).

Some actresses feel that there aren't any challenging roles except the traditional ones. Phyllis Chester, a psychologist, film critic, and the author of *Women and Madness*, disagrees. She suggests that rich film biographies can be made on unusual American women. Two striking examples are Harriet Tubman, the daring abolitionist, and Emma Goldman, the sensational anarchist. "I don't want to see any more films," Chester said in a talk before a cheering audience in 1974, "about women singing the blues!"

Those who support this argument point to television as proof of an audience waiting for new film images of women. The current TV shows present single, independent women able to exist with and not for men. Actresses are shown having brains, ambition, and normal sexual drives. What's more, they are seen as both happy and successful. In the 1974–75 season, for example, of the top fifteen shows in the American national ratings, four starred women: *Rhoda*, *Maude*, *The Mary Tyler Moore Show*, and *Police Woman*. Their popularity made it possible for more female series to go on television. And, as of February 1976, such new shows as *Laverne and Shirley*, *Phyllis*, *The Bionic Woman*, and *One Day at a Time* have allowed women to capture eight of the top twenty television ratings in the country. Equally impressive are the television specials focusing on women, such as *The Autobiography of Miss Jane Pittman* and *Eleanor and Franklin*. In short, the argument is that box-office results need to be understood rather than just reported. Today's audience is opposed to the current film images of women—and not to women themselves.

Before we can better understand the problem of women in American movies, we first need to take a close look at how the Hollywood woman developed. What roles did she play? How did they relate to their times? Who were the great stars that broke through the formula pictures?

Join me now in a brief journey through the past. We may not meet all of your favorite actresses, but we will try to see the best of them. No matter what, it will be a star-studded trip.

CHAPTER 1
SAINTS AND SINNERS

The Hollywood woman got her start in the big city slums at the turn of the century. But why there and then?

Those were the days when a new America was being born. Thousands of people had moved from the country to the cities, where they were joined by millions of European immigrants. In search of a better life, many were soon disappointed. The cities became overcrowded; the surplus of people created a cheap work force. Wages went down. Unemployment went up. Crime increased. As living conditions became more difficult, neighborhoods turned into slums, and by 1900, city life was identified with poverty and vice.

The average male worker spent more than ten hours a day on the job. With little time or energy for travel or organized games, with books and plays too expensive or too difficult, his only solace was the local saloon—there he found escape and enjoyment.

Then came the moving pictures. The new invention cost little to see. Its pictures were exciting and entertaining. What's more, the movies got shown right in the local area. Movies began to compete with the saloons as places to spend leisure hours. Empty stores were turned into movie theaters. A room was darkened, narrow benches set up, people crowded together to view the latest films.

Most women did not attend the first movies. They felt it was dangerous to sit too close to strangers in the dark. Those who did go talked openly of "movie mashers" and "knee flirtation."

Since men made up most of the first movie audiences, the first films treated women as sex objects. Female roles were tied to male fantasies. *Tenderloin at Night* (1899) and *How They Do Things on the Bowery* (1902) showed wicked women drawing country hicks into saloons, drugging their drinks, stealing their money. Even more popular were movies showing women getting undressed. In 1903, for example, a number of films on this subject appeared: *The Corset Maker, The Pajama Girl, The Physical Culture Girl, At the Dressmaker's, From Show Girl to Burlesque Queen.*

The slum theaters worried social reformers who blamed the cities' vices on the movies. It was in the dark theaters, argued the reformers, that the working class learned its bad habits. As a result, do-gooders formed committees to censor movies. Laws were passed stating where, when, and under what conditions movies could be shown.

The reform movement frightened people in the film industry. But what could they do? They disliked making movies only for the poor and the uneducated. They hated the bad name movies had in society. Yet how could they attract a more educated and wealthier audience?

The answer was to become respectable. And the key to respectability was a female audience. Upright, refined family women at the turn of the century were identified with taste and good values. Just as important, such women were good for business. They were almost always escorted by a man or their family. That meant more tickets were sold than with strictly male audiences.

The film makers got the message. They switched their attention to female interests. Heroines began to outnumber heroes in film stories. Scenes of crime or lust were softened or removed. The old values of true love and family were stressed, evil was punished, virtue rewarded. By 1908, daily film attendance reached the 200,000 mark. More than two-thirds of the audience were now women and children. The slogan of the day was "Movies that don't appeal to women, don't make money."

[22]

Such good times made the pioneer film makers greedy. Ten of the most powerful pioneers banded together to form the Motion Picture Patents Company. Known as the Trust, the company claimed it alone had the right to photograph, develop, and print films. Legally, they were right. But the Trust also claimed control over hundreds of film exchanges, companies that rented films to the exhibitors. Here the Trust was wrong. And the film exchanges declared war on the Trust.

Once again women played a key role in the early history of the movies. Carl Laemmle, the head of a big Chicago film exchange and later the founder of Universal Pictures, stumbled on an idea that helped defeat the Trust. He hired one of the Trust's most popular film players to make movies for him. Her name was Florence Lawrence.

Florence Lawrence proved how popular film players could be. The public by the millions now began talking about movie stars as if they were members of the family. Newspapers ran gossip columns. Fan magazines appeared. But Lawrence found little happiness, and her own fame faded quickly. In 1938, while working as a movie extra, she committed suicide.

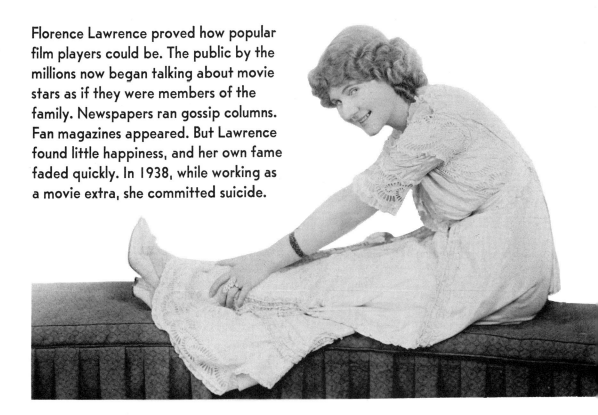

Lawrence was known only as "The Biograph Girl." The first film players never had their names announced; only the studio was publicized. Performers never knew how popular they were and couldn't ask the studio for more money. Laemmle promised to put Lawrence's name in lights. Then, in 1910, he faked a news story that his film player had been killed in a St. Louis street accident. The next day he denied the story, saying that it was a trick by the Trust to destroy him. To prove the truth, he promised that Florence Lawrence would make a public appearance at a St. Louis movie house. When she appeared, she was mobbed by thousands of her fans. And thus the star system was born.

Two years later the star system dealt another death blow to the Trust. Adolph Zukor, a rebel exhibitor and later the founder of Paramount Pictures, felt the time was right for feature, or longer, films. The Trust disagreed. He was not allowed to show anything more than the standard twelve-to fifteen-minute movie. In addition, Zukor bet his future on the idea that stage stars would be as popular with the public as movie stars. Disregarding the Trust, on July 12 he released in New York the French feature film *Queen Elizabeth*. It starred the greatest stage actress of the era: Sarah Bernhardt.

Sarah Bernhardt starred in *Queen Elizabeth* (1912) because she believed it was her one chance for immortality. The great stage actress had grown old, but audiences still adored her. Her fame attracted people who never would have gone to a storefront movie theater.

Although the film was bad, Bernhardt proved to be very popular with movie audiences. Cashing in on his success, Zukor formed a new production company, Famous Players in Famous Plays. Many stage performers who before had refused to work in "the slum movies" now changed their minds. With them came greater profits and more respectability for films.

In 1914, Pearl White, a former medicine show performer, turned from film comedy to movie serials and became a household name around the world. Her first chapter drama was *The Perils of Pauline*. It had twenty separate episodes. Each week, until the end of the serial, the star risked her life to thrill movie audiences. Her daring stunts proved that a movie star needed more than good looks to survive in films.

Pearl White was the most famous of all serial heroines. It was her work that helped movies survive the switch from short to feature films. The first moviemakers felt features were too expensive. Serials were a compromise. Pearl White boasted that she never used stunt women for her dangerous feats. Up to 1915, she was the most popular star in the movies.

Pearl White's courage made her the "Queen of the Serials." At the height of her career, she had more than fifteen million fans in America alone.

The first great movie star, however, was Mary Pickford. She became the most photographed and the best-known woman in the world during the first thirty years of the twentieth century. Between 1909 and 1933 Pickford made more than two hundred movies. Her roles were based on the Cinderella theme—young girls who rose from rags to riches. But "Little Mary" was no weakling or crybaby. She fought hard against evil and prejudice. Yet the girl with golden curls was always sweet, brave, good, and innocent. Her faith in God and a bright future never failed. Pickford movies always had a happy ending, reminding viewers that the old values were best, and consequently, she was known as "America's Sweetheart."

Unlike other stars, Mary Pickford knew her worth to the film industry. By helping set up United Artists in 1919, she began the practice of a performer making and distributing her own movies. Other stars followed suit in the hopes of getting a share of the big profits. During Pickford's prime, she earned more than a million dollars a year.

Pickford's Victorian screen values originated with David Wark Griffith, the first great film director. His heroines stood for beauty, truth, and goodness, and he trained young girls to fit this screen image. In addition to Pickford, he developed such stars as Lillian and Dorothy Gish, Mae Marsh, Blanche Sweet, and Florence Lawrence.

Griffith's movies preached moral lessons. In his monumental film *The Birth of a Nation* (1915), for example, he showed that true love could withstand the racial conflicts of the American Civil War and that a woman's honor had to be protected at all costs. No matter what twists his movies took, Griffith put his heroines at the center of a fight between good and evil.

LILLIAN GISH
AS
ELSIE STONEMAN

MAE MARSH
AS
FLORA CAMERON

MIRIAM COOPER
AS
MARGARET CAMERON

HENRY WALTHALL
AS
COL. BEN CAMERON

RALPH LEWIS
AS
AUSTIN STONEMAN

BN-7

The feature film battle ended with the showing of D. W. Griffith's *The Birth of a Nation* (1915). The story was about two families during and after the American Civil War, the Stonemans were from the North, the Camerons from the South. Their children loved each other, but faced terrible social and racial problems. A great part of the film's popularity was due to the director's great cast. In the middle are Miriam Cooper and Elmer Clifton. After *The Birth of a Nation*, feature films became the standard moving picture.

Born Mary Warne Marsh, Mae Marsh was one of Griffith's most beloved players. In *The Birth of a Nation*, she acted the typical heroine of the early days of film: she giggled, jumped up and down with joy and sweetness, and chose death over dishonor.

Lillian Gish was the silent era's greatest actress and the ideal symbol of young womanhood. For Griffith, Gish and the other stars he directed served to remind the public of the old days. Her finest role, as *True Heart Susie* (1919), is pictured here.

Theda Bara's fame rested on being a *femme fatale*, a woman who destroys men. The real name of the dark-haired, wide-eyed young girl was Theodosia Goodman. William Fox created a brand-new image for her in order to make money for himself. It was the first time a publicity campaign was launched to produce a movie star. Typical of her screen roles is this picture from *Cleopatra* (1918).

Up to 1915, the movie industry worked hard at becoming respectable. Then a change took place. The Trust was defeated, and power shifted to the men who rented films and ran the storefront movie theaters. Such men had grown up in poverty. They did not share America's old values of right and wrong. They felt movies were a business, not a school. Audiences, they claimed, wanted entertainment, not education. Most important, men like Zukor and Laemmle intended to get rich by giving the public what the public wanted.

William Fox, the founder of what would later become Twentieth Century-Fox, showed what the new breed meant by entertainment. He gave the movies its first famous sex star: Theda Bara.

In more than thirty five films between 1915 and 1918, Theda Bara appeared as the most sinful "European" woman alive. She showed audiences what true, noble American women were not. Her roles acted out men's fantasies. Sex and pain were the things she enjoyed most. No man was safe in her presence. She was publicized as "The Vampire," a woman who drains men's lifeblood. Today Theda Bara seems silly and unbelievable, but in her day she was taken seriously. Her success made sex a key element in future female roles.

World War I helped shape how women were portrayed on the screen. The typical film heroine fitted easily into movies about self-sacrifice, loyalty, and patriotism, and the most frequent female roles showed mothers tied to home and family. But the biggest stars were young women, who did their best work as wives and sweethearts. Mary Pickford, for example, helped America's spirits in *The Little American* (1917). She played an American relief worker in neutral Belgium who is almost raped and killed by the German Huns. Picturing the enemy in such an evil light only added to America's desire to enter the war and make the world a safe place to live in.

CHAPTER 2
ENTER HOLLYWOOD

The American film industry changed as it approached the twenties. The day of the small businessman was over. Instead, the industry was ruled by giant organizations headed by such movie tycoons as Zukor, Laemmle, and Fox. The movie industry had become a "vertical system." The men who made the films also rented them and owned the big movie theaters. Their headquarters was Hollywood.

Why there and not in the East where movies started?

Southern California was the perfect choice for many reasons. The movie tycoons needed vast acres of land to build studios and shoot outdoor feature films. California had lots of cheap land. It also had ideal scenery—a nearby ocean, mountain ranges, deserts, and lush countryside—for all types of film stories. What's more, Hollywood had year-round sunshine, perfect for film production. The new studios needed cheap but skilled workers to construct the big stunning sets for feature films. Hollywood had the people to do the job.

For impressionable women, Hollywood seemed the answer to the American dream. And why not? All one needed to become rich and famous was to be a movie star. That didn't require stage experience or talent or money. All you needed, so the fan magazines said, was a lucky break. But you could only be "discovered" in Hollywood.

By 1919, thousands of "movie-struck girls" had invaded southern California. The studios found work for many of them. They became talented film editors like Viola Lawrence, Anne Bauchens, Irene Morra, and Margaret Booth. Many of the best screenwriters were women. Among the more famous were Anita Loos, June Mathis, Frances Marion, Ouida Bergere, Elinor Glyn, and Jeanie MacPherson. Women like Lois Weber and Dorothy Arzner directed movies. Furthermore, the studios employed women dressmakers, set designers, secretaries, mail clerks, and script girls.

Nevertheless, the big dream for the movie-struck girl was to be a star. A few made it to the top because they were friendly with the "right" people. Marion Davies was typical. She became one of the movies' most charming comediennes. But if she hadn't been the mistress of publisher William Randolph Hearst, Davies might never have been in films. Colleen Moore was another. Thanks to her uncle, a powerful Chicago newspaper publisher, she landed a contract with Griffith.

Most women discovered that the key to success in the film world was to forget small-town values. Beauty was prized over brains. A good figure did more for you than a kind heart. Sexual freedom opened more doors than girlish innocence.

Hollywood's social codes were an outgrowth of the nation's new values. The public had tired of restrictions—women, in particular. They had been given the vote, had money to spend, and demanded the fun previously reserved for men only. The swinging chicks of the twenties turned to movies for ideas on how to dress and behave. The movie tycoons ordered their studios to provide those ideas.

No one was more successful at this job than Cecil B. De Mille. His comedies and melodramas perfected the art of "sex appeal" in movies. One of his specialties was the bathroom scene. No matter what the story was about, De Mille always had a scene that allowed the actress to bathe herself. In sensational stories about the upper class, he also explored bedroom adventures and the latest fashions.

But De Mille was careful not to offend traditional values. Wicked women were always punished, broken marriages were mended in the last reel. He kept reminding the public

that smart people know just how far to go without getting hurt.

His most famous star was Gloria Swanson. She became the first movie queen to show sexual sophistication. Her De Mille films set the tone for the early twenties. Glamour and temptation were her trademarks. More often than not, she starred as a newly married woman who ignored her marriage contract. Together, De Mille and Swanson affected not only America's moral values, but also its female fashions. Flappers everywhere dressed and wore their hair according to the styles shown in the latest Swanson movie.

Marion Davies was sixteen and a Ziegfeld Follies girl when she began her love affair with fifty-eight-year-old William Randolph Hearst. The powerful newspaper tycoon forced her on the movie public. She is seen at left with Nils Asther in *The Cardboard Lover* (1928). Below: Cecil B. De Mille's *Male and Female* (1919), which dealt with a rich woman falling in love with her butler, shocked America. Gloria Swanson played the adulteress.

Lillian Gish was another star who kept sex and passion in the background. In *Way Down East* (1920), she and D. W. Griffith proved that the public still valued the old social code. As the twenties wore on, however, Gish's gentle beauty no longer appealed to fans more interested in sexy heroines.

For those movie fans who cherished the old values there was still Mary Pickford. Twice in the twenties she tried to play adult roles, but the films died at the box office. Thus the public "forced" her to remain childlike in films like *Little Annie Rooney* (1925).

Just as interesting to American audiences in the twenties was Hollywood's image of the European woman. Moviemakers pictured her as a symbol of passion and sin. Foreign actresses were featured in emotion-packed love stories that depicted a passion unthinkable in the films of Mary Pickford and Lillian Gish. Among the most famous European actresses were Pola Negri and Greta Garbo.

Pola Negri was the first European actress to become a Hollywood star. Zukor brought her to Paramount in the hope that she would become the leading movie vamp. But Negri was more than just a sex symbol. She was a fine dramatic actress. In film after film, she showed that worldly women suffered as much as they loved. Unfortunately, Hollywood had little use for her offscreen contractual demands and stormy love affairs. By the end of the decade, she found herself unwelcome in the movie capital.

Pola Negri, was admired as "the worldly woman." Her offscreen, well-publicized romances with Charles Chaplin and Rudolph Valentino helped her to succeed at the box office. In this still from *The Cheat* (1923), she is being branded by Charles De Roche.

Greta Garbo was a different story. She never lost touch with her audiences. Although brought to America to become a Hollywood vamp, the young Swedish star refused to be limited by her screen roles. Garbo's great beauty and inspired acting won her fans around the world. Sometimes she played a fallen woman who asks for nothing and suffers all the pain that men can give. At other times, she acted the role of a troubled woman who survives with the aid of a powerful unseen force. But always, Garbo was the woman who lived for love.

Greta Garbo proved to be the timeless star. Audiences found in her the perfect lover. In *Flesh and the Devil* (1926), Garbo was a doomed wife whose love for another man leads to tragedy. John Gilbert played the part of her lover.

The director who best captured America's distorted image of the European mood was Erich von Stroheim. In such films as *Blind Husbands* (1919) and *Foolish Wives* (1922) he used a basic plot, in which a silly, wealthy woman is tempted into sin by a lustful European. But before any sexual transgression occurs, the erring female is saved from disgrace. What made his movies so timely was von Stroheim's modern approach to marriage. He pointed out that marriages broke up because husbands ignored their wives. Like De Mille, von Stroheim showed that lonely married women appealed to immoral men. The difference between the two directors was that von Stroheim's women had more depth.

Everywhere you went in the twenties in America, cheaply made sex movies were also showing. The titles of the films told you what to expect: *A Shocking Night, Their Mutual Child, A Virgin Paradise, The Good-Bad Wife,* and *The Way Women Love.*

Reformers were horrified. The promise of getting rich quickly had made Hollywood "The New Babylon." The streets were filled with prostitutes, gamblers, thieves, and blackmailers. Bootleggers and dope peddlers grew rich by satisfying the wants of the fun-loving population. Reformers appeared helpless. It seemed as if movies were too big and too powerful to stop.

A series of film scandals, starting in late 1921, turned the tide. Famous screen comic Roscoe "Fatty" Arbuckle was accused of raping and killing a young starlet. Popular stars Mabel Normand and Mary Miles Minter were tied to the murder of a noted director. Actor Wallace Reid, "The All-American Boy," died as the result of his drug habits. Headlines across the nation declared that Hollywood was the city of sin.

The public was outraged. Reformers seized their chance. They switched their attacks to the stars themselves. These people, argued the critics, were acting as role models for

America's youth. These stars were our children's culture heroes. If the young people were to be saved from a life of sin, the movies needed to be censored. "The public has to be protected" was the battle cry.

To protect themselves and their million-dollar investments, movie tycoons hired the Postmaster General of the United States, Will H. Hays. His job was "to clean up the movies." Studio heads formed a group called the Motion Picture Producers and Distributors Association. Known as the Hays Office, its job was to reform the industry from within. By 1927, a list of "Don'ts and Be Carefuls" was in force. Good taste, for example, had to be used in movies showing women and men in bed together, the deliberate seduction of girls, and the institution of marriage.

The self-reform movement might have won if film profits hadn't dropped in the late twenties. Searching for a solution, the film tycoons turned to talking pictures in 1927. They borrowed heavily to remodel their silent studios and movie houses to accommodate sound films. The need for money forced the film makers to ignore Hays and turn back to the one surefire box-office attraction: sex.

The renewed interest in "having fun" gave Hollywood two of its brightest stars: Clara Bow and Joan Crawford.

Joan Crawford is often credited as the star who most teen-agers imitated in the twenties. Her best roles featured her as an ambitious flapper out to make a place for herself in the social world. In *Our Dancing Daughters* (1928), she summarized the decade's love for glamorous and free living.

Clara Bow was the first movie queen to make sex appeal believable. Beautiful to look at and wild at heart, Bow acted the role of the working girl out to snare a rich husband. She laughed. She danced on tabletops. But if men thought her "loose," she set them straight. Known as the "It Girl," Clara Bow was the image of sex appeal.

Joan Crawford was another new star who glorified youth and beauty. Like Bow, she was a true rags-to-riches story. Each had been a poor girl who won a movie contest and wound up in films. But, unlike Bow, Crawford remained a star for decades. She had the ability to play more than flapper parts. Her strength was in portraying unbeatable women. The Crawford character always survived.

The importance of women to movies in the twenties cannot be emphasized enough. By the end of the decade, studios were specializing in the "woman's movie." Like today's soap operas on television, the woman's movie focused on

Clara Bow had the biggest audience appeal in the twenties. Between 1925 and 1930 she played the "party girl" who was actually pure and innocent. In *Wings* (1929), Bow was the hometown girl working in Paris as an ambulance driver during World War I.

One of the most popular themes in the "woman's movie" is the sacrifice of a mother for her children. In *Madame X* (1929), Ruth Chatterton decides to spare her son pain by keeping from him her true identity.

sex and female suffering. Typical of the type was *Madame X* (1929). In the film Ruth Chatterton plays a woman who leaves her husband for another man. When she discovers her son is ill, she returns only to be turned out by her un-forgiving spouse. From then on her life goes downhill. Years later she kills a man who intends to blackmail her family. Her son becomes her lawyer not knowing she is his mother. Rather than let him find out her true identity, she confesses to the crime.

The woman's movie hinted at the problems facing women in society. Men might like smart, glamorous companions, but not as wives. In reality, marriage meant babies and housework, not fun and good times. More jobs might be open to women, but they were almost always at poor and unequal salaries. If one thing was clear in 1929, it was that men ruled the country and the movies.

Gloria Swanson was one of the first stars to try to break away from male control. After her successful films with C. B. De Mille, she set up her own production company in 1927. Her gift for romance and mystery was clear in the 1928 movie *Sadie Thompson* (below). As the fallen woman who survives disgrace and rape, Swanson won the first of her three Academy Award nominations. Lionel Barrymore played the reformer who attacked her and then committed suicide. Left: the end of an era came when Mary Pickford finally cut her curls in 1928. Tired of playing innocent children, the thirty-five-year-old star wanted a new image. Her mistake was that she became just another leading lady. In *The Taming of the Shrew* (1929), Pickford teamed with her husband, Douglas Fairbanks, hoping to regain their fading popularity. But by 1933 her twenty-four-year career was ended.

CHAPTER 3
FAME AND FORTUNE

The Hollywood woman underwent sweeping changes in the thirties.

It started with the sound revolution. By 1930, many silent screen stars had failed to switch successfully to the "talkies." Among the more famous were Pola Negri, Clara Bow, Gloria Swanson, Lillian Gish, and Mary Pickford. Some had never learned to act. Their fame had rested on their physical beauty alone. Others had bad movie voices; they didn't sound the way they looked. Some, too rich to care about learning new methods of film acting, retired. Others couldn't shed their "flapper" or "child-woman" images.

The failure of so many actresses brought forth a new type of screen star. She had to be able to act. Directors could no longer talk to her during the shooting of a scene. The sound cameras picked up any noise on the set. Talkies made characters more lifelike. Performers had to be able to handle dialogue, to speak and to act realistically. Many of the new stars, therefore, came from Broadway. Some of the best were Katharine Hepburn, Bette Davis, Barbara Stanwyck, and Joan Blondell.

The radical changes in society also affected the fortunes of the Hollywood woman. The collapse of the stock market in late 1929 had started the Great Depression. By the early thirties an economic plague was sweeping across the country. Banks closed. Factories shut down. Unemployment skyrocketed to the fifteen-million mark. In the richest country in the world people were walking around homeless and hungry.

Thus the first talkies tried to give women relief from the

harsh realities of their everyday life. Musicals were the rage. Stories about poor girls who found fame and fortune on the stage served two purposes. First, musicals amused audiences with the novelty of all-talking, all-singing films. But second and more important, it turned the Hollywood woman into a glamour queen. She wore stunning gowns and traded wisecracks with the opposite sex. Musicals stressed that success depended upon a woman's using her brains. Of course, the glamourous stars weren't 'real,' but they did provide jobless women and tired housewives with a form of escape. For a few hours at least, a woman could daydream about fancy clothes, she could fantasize about a more exciting life.

The first talkies also reminded women of their roles as sex objects in a man's world. Nowhere was this more clearly shown than in the Depression's gangster films. Studios turned the daily headlines about bloody gang wars into blistering movies about the underworld. Women played a special part in every mobster's life. As "Little Caesar" or "Scarface" rose to the top, he found a sexy gun moll urging him on. She went along with the easy money and the high living. But in reality, the women in such movies acted as a prize, not a person.

Such roles only pointed out women's helplessness in society. The Depression made it clear that men were considered more important. Women couldn't belong to unions, didn't receive equal pay for the same work done by men, and marriage eliminated them from certain teaching positions if a man needed the same job. By the end of the thirties, more than 20 percent of all working women were unemployed.

Yet it was that sense of helplessness that gave the Hollywood woman her first of two golden ages in the decade.

Studio heads wisely decided to put their glamour queens in Depression roles. The idea was to show them living in poverty and shame. One of the most memorable stars to

Greta Garbo became one of Hollywood's most famous legends during the thirties. So great was her talent that she influenced not only styles of clothing but also schools of acting. In *Susan Lenox: Her Fall and Rise* (1931), she played a woman of destiny. Clark Gable played her lover.

take this path was Greta Garbo. Her first talkie, *Anna Christie* (1930), outlined the pattern for movies about "helpless women." Playing the part of a waterfront tramp, Garbo showed why some women turn to such a life and created sympathy for the many jobless people who were forced to do things they hated. With her husky voice, Garbo also caught the tone of the tough Depression woman. Typical were her instructions to a bartender, "Give me a whiskey, ginger ale on the side, and don't be stingy, baby."

The following year in *Susan Lenox: Her Fall and Rise*, Garbo refined her new image. She became a girl who falls from respectability to ruin. Susan Lenox stood for many women trying to survive in a society gone crazy. She suffered so that others might be saved, and in the end, Susan was reunited with her loved one. The ability to endure became the Garbo trademark. She made inner dignity worth fighting for. And sex was seen as only a means to an end. Men might abuse a woman, but they couldn't destroy her spirit.

Another European star who shared the hard life with Garbo was Marlene Dietrich. Like Garbo, she enchanted men with her beauty. But unlike Garbo's women, Dietrich's were more intelligent. She saw men as weak and cruel. If sex was the name of the game, the Dietrich character played it tough and out in the open. A man could have what he wanted, but only for the right price.

During the Depression, Marlene Dietrich rivaled Garbo in popularity. Both were glamorous stars who specialized in being mysterious women. Unlike Garbo, however, Dietrich owed part of her fame to a director, Josef von Sternberg. Study this shot from *Blonde Venus* (1932) to see how much the lighting, costume, and composition add to the star's characterization.

The difference between the two stars when playing "fallen women" was most evident in Dietrich's 1932 film *Blonde Venus*. Like Susan Lenox, Helen Faraday sacrificed her respectability for someone she loved. Both were victims, yet Helen never pitied herself. She met life as it happened. Her plan was to control the men who desired her. She schemed, made demands, and in the end she won on her terms.

The Hollywood woman had more than one image to give unhappy people in the early thirties. Equally popular were the spicy, down-to-earth blonde bombshells. The best of them included Carole Lombard, Ginger Rogers, Alice Faye, and Marion Davies. But two were particularly outstanding.

The first was Jean Harlow. She made active sex her business. It made no difference whom she loved. He could be married or single, rich or poor. The idea was to have fun. Some women resented her lack of principles. But men adored the wisecracking, gum-chewing star. They flocked to her lusty films. She wore no underclothes and her reveal-

Jean Harlow, the hard-boiled sex symbol of the Depression, knew what she wanted and how to get it. This still is from *Red Dust* (1932).

Mae West remains one of the most remarkable women in film history. She was desired by men, but her own desires were more important. This still is from *She Done Him Wrong* (1933).

ing dresses excited the male audiences. She played on the fact that they thought the worst of her. Even Harlow's harsh, scratchy voice won her fans. It made her seem more earthy. She became the Depression's best sex symbol.

Just how much she was a man's woman was shown in *Red Dust* (1932). Set on a rubber plantation in Indochina, this hot romance starred Harlow as a promiscuous lady fleeing from the law. At first Clark Gable avoids her. Then she turns on her charms. By the film's end, he belongs to her. Hard but kind, common but lovable, Harlow proved a woman could take care of herself. It was a message Depression women enjoyed.

The other great blonde bombshell was Mae West. Like Harlow and Dietrich, she was a realist about sex. But unlike them, she made it a joke. The West character kidded audiences about sexual taboos. She reversed the standard male-female relationships. Mae West chose her lovers instead of being chosen. She called the shots, not the male leads. Outspoken and crude, she had no equal in film history. Reformers throughout the nation were shocked by her films, while the public by the millions loved her boldness.

In her most famous role, as Lady Lou in *She Done Him Wrong* (1933), she reduced men to little boys. She advised timid girls that "When women go wrong, men go right after them." For one of the few times in screen history, it was the woman who loved and left. Seen from today's viewpoint, Mae West was one of the most radically innovative women ever to grace the silver screen.

For a while the great studios seemed untouched by the Great Depression. Thanks in large part to the popularity of female stars box-office profits soared. In 1930, for example, ninety million people went to the movies each week, more than half the total population of the United States. But as times grew tougher, the figures began to drop. In 1931, weekly attendance dipped to seventy-five million; in 1932, sixty million. But even then, American families saw a film on the average of three times a week.

Fighting the sagging box office in their usual manner, studios increased sex and violence in movies. They attacked the old social codes. And the Hollywood woman, enjoying her greatest freedom, became more outspoken, more daring in her actions.

Will Hays, the industry-appointed censor, shook his head in horror. He warned that Hollywood was headed for serious trouble. No one listened. He convinced the industry to adopt in 1930 a new movie code, which attempted to tone down sex and violence in films. But the movie companies only gave token acceptance to the new Motion Picture Production Code. More often than not, the producers did as they wanted.

There seemed to be a good reason why the studios ignored Hays. The talkies had forced the old film tycoons, like Fox and Laemmle, to borrow large sums of money. The stock-market crash had made them powerless to repay their giant debts. As a result, a new breed of moneymen took over control of the studios. Mostly wealthy investors from Wall Street, these new people shared the same goal as the men they replaced: to make as much money as possible. Sex and violence seemed the answer.

Then came 1933. The Depression reached Hollywood. Almost one-third of all American movie houses closed. Fox, Paramount, Universal, and Radio-Keith-Orpheum (RKO) faced financial ruin. The industry was on the verge of disaster.

The Roman Catholic Church now saw its chance to reform Hollywood. For more than thirty years crusading groups had tried and failed. But in 1933 Catholics made up one-third of the nation's sixty million churchgoers, and these worshipers listened to their clergymen. If attendance at a movie was forbidden by the Roman Catholic Church, most Catholics didn't go.

Deciding to clean up the movies, American Catholic bishops formed an organization called the Legion of Decency. Its job was to decide which films were decent and which were not. Those that got a bad rating were then boycotted by Catholics. Other religious groups quickly joined with the Catholic bishops.

By 1934 the Roman Catholic Church had won the fight. They had shown Hollywood that "bad" films meant bad profits. A peace treaty was made between the reformers and the industry. Both sides agreed that movies had become a mirror of the nation's culture and values. But from 1934 on, movies had to set a higher moral standard for the nation. Marriage, for example, had to be respected. Passion should be discouraged. Crime couldn't be glorified. Good should never lose to evil. Any character who did something wrong had to be punished or reformed by the last reel.

To insure that Hollywood would keep its word to reform, Joseph Breen was named head of the revamped Production

Code Administration. Power was now centered here rather than in the Hays office. Breen was a tough Catholic and an ex-journalist. His powers over the movies were unlimited. Scripts needed his approval. Every finished movie needed to be seen by his office before it could be released. And even films in general release could be recalled if he felt something was wrong with their contents.

The Breen Office, of course, forced a change in the Hollywood woman. It took the sting out of the blonde bombshell. It toned down the fallen woman images created by Garbo and Dietrich. Stars began wearing more conservative clothes. They changed their vocabularies. Marriage became more popular than affairs.

Starting in 1934, the Hollywood woman began her second golden age.

Claudette Colbert signaled the start of a new and more sentimental movie heroine. In *Imitation of Life* (1934), for example, she played a working-class widow who becomes a rich pancake manufacturer. Her personal pleasure is sacrificed for her daughter's happiness. That same year Colbert mixed sentiment with comedy in *It Happened One Night*. This time she was a runaway heiress who winds up with he-man reporter Clark Gable. Sexual taboos were strictly followed, and no criticism was made of traditional values.

Claudette Colbert made a surprise hit in movie comedies during the mid-thirties. Both she and co-star Clark Gable had given their studios trouble. As a result, they were sent to work for a poor company named Columbia. The film they made was *It Happened One Night* (1934). Directed by Frank Capra, it won all five major Academy Awards, including Oscars for Colbert and Gable.

[55]

Bette Davis's battles for better parts made history at Warner Brothers. Because of her talent and guts, she proved actresses weren't tied to any one image. Davis's first big break came in *Of Human Bondage* (1934). Leslie Howard was the man she tormented.

As box-office figures climbed, studios jumped on the respectability bandwagon. Stars were cast in movie versions of popular and classic novels. Culture was one more way of improving the industry's new image. It also gave the studios a chance to show the public how sex could be dry-cleaned.

RKO illustrated the method in its 1934 screen version of W. Somerset Maugham's autobiographical novel, *Of Human Bondage*. The film focused on a tortuous love affair between Philip Carey, a clubfooted medical student (Leslie Howard), and Mildred Rogers, a seductive waitress (Bette Davis). The studio took pains to show how the "new" film morality operated. Passionate lovemaking was avoided. The sexual power that Mildred had over Philip was not shown as

Vivien Leigh was visiting Hollywood in 1938 when she was unexpectedly given the most famous female role in the history of movies: Scarlett O'Hara in *Gone With the Wind*. Clark Gable played Rhett Butler.

"attractive or alluring." Because of Mildred's evil ways, she spent a considerable amount of screen time suffering. In the end, she dies for her sins. The same events took place in the novel, but in conforming to the Production Code, RKO gave more weight to them in the film.

Other screen adaptations of famous books followed suit. Sex was played down or sanitized. Irene Dunne made a big hit as a beautiful woman first blinded and then cured by a reformed playboy in *Magnificent Obsession* (1935). Vivien Leigh gave a new look to career women of another era in *Gone with the Wind* (1939). And Judy Garland gained everlasting fame as the young girl lost in *The Wizard of Oz* (1939). Such movies won over audiences by their glamorous sets, famous stars, and well-publicized stories.

By 1937, the Hollywood woman was once more respectable. For that matter so was the industry. *A Star Is Born* (1937) went out of its way to show how tough it was to reach the top. Janet Gaynor played a film-struck girl who reaches stardom at the expense of personal happiness.

Hollywood also began reshaping the nation's values. President Franklin Roosevelt called for hope and courage and asked America to believe in its future. The movie industry supported these goals by having its stars provide role models.

Bette Davis was one such culture heroine. She had begun the decade as a tough blonde babe. But as the country changed, so did her image. Now she played women whose passions destroyed them. Sex and ambition brought her characters pain and destruction.

Typical of her evil woman image was *Jezebel* (1938). Davis played a vicious southern belle who would stop at nothing to get what she wanted. She proved just how dangerous passion was. But Davis also proved how talent had replaced beauty as a basis for stardom. From the mid-thirties on, she became one of Hollywood's most enduring and gifted actresses.

Above: in the thirties, Janet Gaynor replaced Mary Pickford as America's sweetheart. Wholesomeness was her trademark. It was no accident, therefore, that she was so convincing as the film-struck girl who found fame in *A Star Is Born* (1937). Center: *Jezebel* (1938) was the first of many films to show the range of the Bette Davis talent. Legend has it she took the part to show producer David O. Selznick that she should play Scarlett O'Hara. Below: Claudette Colbert entered movies as a sexy vamp, but soon switched to playing above-average women. In *Imitation of Life* (1934), she put motherhood and family goals on Hollywood's new priority list.

[58]

Katharine Hepburn was one of the few stars who made Hollywood change for her. Unhappy at RKO, she bought up her contract and hired out to Columbia to make *Holiday* (1938). The story found her fighting with Doris Nolan over Cary Grant. Hepburn's role argued that no one had a right to run another person's life.

The talkies ushered in a tough, professional Hollywood woman. No one fitted the description better than Jean Arthur. In *Mr. Deeds Goes to Town* (1936), she gave Gary Cooper the courage to make his dreams come true.

Katharine Hepburn was another famous role model for Americans. Her film parts thrilled working women. She proved "manly traits" belonged to females as well. The Hepburn character was independent, she wisecracked, she was ambitious, she was professional. And she made a good wife. Men saw in her an equal.

Her best roles were in comedies. In *Holiday* (1938), as a stubborn society girl who falls in love with her sister's fiance, Hepburn charmed men and women alike. She set the standards that future screen acting would be judged by.

But the lady who most caught the spirit of Hollywood's new role was Jean Arthur. She became the thirties' symbol of idealism and sentiment. Her roles featured the star as a good-natured working woman who never lost hope. Guided by the genius of director Frank Capra, she always spoke for the people. Jean Arthur attacked false leaders, fought against corrupt businessmen, and her boyfriends were always everyday people who dreamed of making America better.

Mr. Deeds Goes to Town (1936) captured the heart of the Arthur character. Playing the role of a big-city reporter who helps an idealistic Gary Cooper beat corrupt moneymen, Arthur revealed human and sentimental qualities. The film pointed out how people sometimes misjudge and distrust good individuals. But in the end the Arthur character showed that everyday Americans were the best hope for the country's future.

As the decade ended, the Hollywood woman still led the movie parade. Her first golden age had started with the likes of Garbo, Dietrich, Harlow, and West. Their roles had challenged traditional values. They had given women a new look. When the movie industry switched its loyalties, Colbert, Hepburn, Davis, and Arthur took charge. But no matter what the issues, the public continued to adore the female stars.

CHAPTER 4
LOST VICTORIES

The forties were Hollywood's best and most troublesome years. The decade began badly, and ended even worse. Yet the in-between years cloaked the industry and its stars in glory.

The seeds of trouble were planted long before America entered World War II on December 8, 1941. The Depression years had turned Hollywood into a political battlefield. Europe's spreading war was the hot issue.

One part of the industry argued that political propaganda films were bad business. Foreign nations, for example, supplied the industry with 30 percent of its profits. Movies attacking the rise of Nazism endangered those profits. Even closer to home, America's official position was to stay neutral as Hitler waged war in Europe; to make anti-Nazi films was, therefore, unpatriotic, for such films undermined national policy. In fact, by the start of the forties, isolationist congressmen were investigating Hollywood's "anti-American" activities.

But another part of Hollywood—those who felt the industry had a moral responsibility—refused to be frightened. Films, they argued, should educate and inform, the nation should "see" Adolf Hitler's anti-Semitism. The American public should know about the fascist overthrow of the Spanish government. The country should be warned about dangers to democratic life in the U.S.A.

The Hollywood woman, of course, was used by both Hollywood camps. Judy Garland was cast in such "escapist" films as *Andy Hardy Meets the Debutante* (1940).

The popular Andy Hardy series showed that American kids could do and go where they pleased. Katharine Hepburn also championed the democratic way in *The Philadelphia Story* (1940). Her typical role cheered American individualism. But other films used the Hollywood woman for political propaganda. For example, Paulette Goddard appeared as a helpless Jewish heroine in *The Great Dictator* (1940), and Jean Arthur fought against a fascist politician in *Meet John Doe* (1941).

Warm, pretty, and carefree, Paulette Goddard was one of the forties' most popular stars. In *The Great Dictator* (1940), she played a Jewish girl beloved by Charles Chaplin. The film satirized Hitler.

Japan's attack on Pearl Harbor on December 7, 1941, seemed to settle the issue. With America at war, Hollywood became part of the general mobilization for victory. Only after World War II would the internal political battles resume, and then, as we shall see, the results proved disastrous.

The Hollywood woman, in the meantime, did her share for the war effort. She visited servicemen in training camps and at the front. She took part in war bond drives. Led by Bette Davis, she even ran The Hollywood Canteen, a special social club for servicemen. Every evening a famous band played music while the boys danced with Hollywood stars like Hedy Lamarr and Betty Grable. The latter boosted the boys' morale by mailing sexy pictures of herself to servicemen everywhere. These pictures, hung in the men's lockers, crowned Grable as "The Pinup Queen of the Forties."

The Hollywood woman also set out to educate the nation to its common enemies, its allies, and to life overseas. Greer Garson, for example, in *Mrs. Miniver* (1942), showed how mothers and housewives suffered in war-torn England. That same year Ingrid Bergman in *Casablanca* reminded audiences that patriotism was more important than personal happiness. Other stars performed in films depicting the dangers presented by the fascists in Italy and the warlords in Japan.

The Hollywood woman, in addition, found herself in other wartime roles. Priscilla Lane fought at home against Nazi spies in *Saboteur* (1942). Paulette Goddard was the brave nurse trapped on a Pacific island by advancing Japanese troops in *So Proudly We Hail* (1943). Tallulah Bankhead was the shipwrecked heroine in *Lifeboat* (1944). And Loretta Young led a group of women who delivered aircraft to battle zones in *Ladies Courageous* (1944).

But by 1943, servicemen began asking for less propaganda and more entertainment. They knew what war was all

In *Mrs. Miniver* (1942), Greer Garson played the ideal mother and wife during wartime. The Garson character kept her courage and always had a sense of fun. To millions of troubled people, Garson was an inspiration. It was no surprise, therefore, that the Miniver role won the star an Oscar in 1942. Walter Pidgeon was her tired husband.

about. What they didn't know was how things were back home. They wanted actresses who reminded them of Mother, the girl next door, and their wives. The demand was for the old formula films—musicals, melodramas, mysteries.

The movie musical answered the call. Betty Grable brought back the good old days in the turn-of-the-century romance *Coney Island* (1943). Rita Hayworth delighted servicemen when she sang "Long Ago and Far Away" in the spectacular *Cover Girl* (1944). Hollywood even made a musical to improve race relations, as when Lena Horne and Ethel Waters starred in the all-black film *Cabin in the Sky* (1943).

Ethel Waters (left) and Lena Horne were two women who boosted the morale of black servicemen during World War II. *Cabin in the Sky* (1943) was a silly fable about good and evil fighting for the soul of Eddie "Rochester" Anderson (middle). It was only one more example of the limited parts open to blacks.

Romantic melodramas explored the sacrifices war wives and waiting women made on the homefront. Ginger Rogers in *Tender Comrade* (1943) identified with working women, enacting the long hours spent at a munitions plant, showing how wives shared daily problems, and demonstrating a widow's courage when given the tragic news of her husband's death in combat. Bette Davis was another inspirational woman in *Watch on the Rhine* (1943). She sacrifices first her husband and then her sons to destroy Nazism. And Claudette Colbert symbolized the ideal war wife in *Since You Went Away* (1944). She keeps her children, Shirley Temple and Jennifer Jones, mindful of their duty.

In some ways Hollywood benefited from the war. While production in other industries was restricted, movies were left alone. President Roosevelt felt films were needed for morale. Women, in particular, used them for escape. The war had put almost twenty million women to work in jobs formerly held by men; they dug coal, built tanks, and produced munitions. Often these jobs required three eight-hour shifts. Tired and alone, women went to the movies. To meet the needs of the various work shifts, many movie houses stayed open around the clock seven days a week. It was no surprise, therefore, that weekly attendance during the war reached 100 million people a week.

America's war effort did, however, affect how movies were made. Gas rationing reduced the distance directors could travel to shoot a film, and as a result, movies took on a more cramped look. Critical shortages developed in such things as wood, metal, and raw film stock. The stunning sets of old were more difficult to build. The use of electricity was tightly budgeted, and the consequent limited lighting gave films a more sinister appearance.

Such production shortages, understandably, influenced the types of films made. Psychological thrillers—stories about people trapped by fear and mental illness—became popular. The main characters seemed helpless to protect

In the thirties, Barbara Stanwyck played tough, wisecracking females. But in the forties she switched to evil roles. In *Double Indemnity* (1944) she became a murderous woman who persuades foolish Fred MacMurray to kill her husband. Her portrayal of this selfish woman won Stanwyck her third Oscar nomination.

themselves; they found it hard to know who their friends and enemies were; they moved about in dark, ugly worlds—evil seemed everywhere.

Female stars were featured in these psychological thrillers. Most of the famous male stars had gone into the service and the industry found it hard to replace them during the war. As a result, movie scripts focused more on actresses.

One type of role played by the Hollywood woman in psychological thrillers stressed evil. The star was ruled by greed. She was willing to do anything to get what she wanted. Barbara Stanwyck created the ideal Evil Woman in *Double Indemnity* (1944), when she persuaded her insurance man to murder her husband. Only afterward did the hoodwinked Fred MacMurray realize he was to be her next victim. "How could I know," he explains, "that murder sometimes smells like honeysuckle?"

Another role in such thrillers was the Helpless Woman who found herself tormented by an evil man. Here the star became the victim. She didn't know whom to trust. Ingrid Bergman played the symbolic victim in *Gaslight* (1944). Throughout the suspenseful story her husband tries to drive her insane. At the end, of course, she is saved when the tables are turned and her husband is trapped. When he pleads for help, she responds by telling him, ''I hate you! Without a shred of pity, without a shred of regret, I watch you go with glory in my heart.''

Ingrid Bergman beat out Stanwyck for the Oscar in 1944 as the terrified housewife in *Gaslight* **(shown here with Angela Lansbury and Charles Boyer).**

The end of World War II pressed the Hollywood woman into new roles. Joan Crawford in *Mildred Pierce* (1945) showed that career women did not lead happy lives. Myrna Loy revealed the problems that wives faced with ex-soldiers in *The Best Years of Our Lives* (1946). Veronica Lake showed the troubles facing unfaithful wives of returning servicemen in *The Blue Dahlia* (1946).

Joan Crawford in *Mildred Pierce* (1945) summed up the "woman's film" during the forties. As a middle-class housewife who sacrifices love and happiness for her corrupt daughter, Crawford revealed that motherhood wasn't always fun. Ann Blyth played the vicious daughter.

Rita Hayworth was the sex goddess of the forties. With the exception of Betty Grable, she was the most famous pin-up queen of World War II. Hayworth's greatest moment in movies came when she sang the teasing song "Put the Blame on Mame" in the film *Gilda* (1946).

These realistic dramas were not typical. The big emphasis was still on escape movies, and sex stars were once again popular. The best of the day, Rita Hayworth, symbolized the mood of the times. By the mid-forties she had switched from high-class musicals to such sex thrillers as *Gilda* (1946), in which she played the wife of a South American gambler who resumes her passion for ex-boyfriend Glenn Ford. Her stress on physical sex reminded audiences of Harlow and Dietrich.

In early 1947 few realized that Hollywood was on the verge of disaster. But inflation was everywhere. A housing crisis existed. Bills and debts for everyone were running high. Women had lost most of their jobs to returning servicemen. The birthrate was increasing, and a "baby boom" was under way. Couples began staying home, using radio and the new toy television for amusement. Hollywood suddenly found movie attendance dropping. All these events cut down profits.

Even more disastrous to Hollywood was government interference. The Justice Department had won a long-standing battle to divorce studios from movie theater ownership. Begun in the thirties, by the late forties the battle was over. Producers lost control of film distribution. They were no longer sure that the movies they made would make money at the box office. The U.S. Congress also resumed its look into Hollywood's political values. The House Un-American Activities Committee claimed the movie industry was filled with communists. The industry, frightened and cowardly, set up a "blacklist." Anyone even suspected of being a communist could not find work. In short, Hollywood panicked.

Desperate, the studios turned once again to realism, and once again the Helpless Woman formula was recycled. Barbara Stanwyck played a bedridden woman who accidently discovers she is to be murdered in *Sorry, Wrong Number* (1948). Olivia de Havilland became a sick woman placed in an overcrowded mental institution in *The Snake Pit* (1948). Jane Wyman gave an Oscar-winning performance as a deaf-mute brutally raped in *Johnny Belinda* (1948).

Movies featuring women also explored human rights during the late forties. Jeanne Crain focused on the problems of a light-skinned black woman trying to be white in *Pinky* (1949). Star-turned-producer Ida Lupino examined the pressures facing unwed mothers in *Not Wanted* (1949). Katharine Hepburn ridiculed the idea that women were inferior to men in *Adam's Rib* (1949).

But nothing seemed to work. Attendance at the movies continued to drop. Profits fell further. Studios began making fewer feature films. Hundreds of movie houses closed. And this was only the beginning of Hollywood's downhill slide.

Barbara Stanwyck again switched her image in *Sorry, Wrong Number* (1948). This time she was the naive wife who accidentally overhears her husband's plan to murder her. It was her last great performance and won the star her fourth and final Oscar nomination.

Barbara Stanwyck lost the Best Actress award in 1948 to Jane Wyman (left). The wide-eyed, baby-faced Wyman turned in a convincing performance as the deaf-mute who is raped by the town bully. But when the same man tries to take her child away, she kills him. *Johnny Belinda* (1948) helped Wyman replace Irene Dunne as the star of sob-story melodramas for the next decade. Jeanne Crain (center) typified the girl-next-door heroine in the forties. Only rarely did Twentieth Century-Fox let her try a demanding part. In *Pinky* (1949) Crain played a black woman trying to pass for white. At right: Katharine Hepburn and Spencer Tracy were husband and wife lawyers taking opposing sides in *Adam's Rib* (1949). The issue was over the rights of a neglected wife and a mistreated mother. Once again Hepburn was fighting for the rights of women.

CHAPTER 5
MOVING BACKWARD

By 1950 the message was clear. Hollywood's very survival was in doubt. Television, the new national pastime, was keeping millions of people at home and away from movie houses. Industry profits were 75 percent below what they had been in 1947. Studios were rushing to cut expenses everywhere; almost 50 percent of the stars had lost their contracts; close to 25 percent of the screenwriters were out of jobs. The studio structure that had been around since the early twenties was coming to an end.

America's political climate also gave Hollywood nightmares. The "Red Scare" was everywhere. The nation was engaged in a limited war in Korea. Congress was still investigating communist activities in the movie industry. Producers turning out films critical of the nation's problems were dubbed "un-American." Many liberal artists lost their jobs or left to find work overseas.

To protect themselves, the big studios—Paramount, M-G-M, RKO, Twentieth Century-Fox, Warner Brothers, Columbia—looked backward. They turned to the old formula movies for help. Crime stories, romances, musicals, westerns, and women's movies took over production schedules. The big studios also turned to gimmicks. Just as the novelty of sound brought fans back to movies, so the novelty of 3-D films, Cinerama, and Cinemascope helped in the fifties. Thus the industry fought to stay alive by stressing entertainment—and avoiding controversy.

Women found little to praise in these times. The climate in the country stressed male superiority. Females were discouraged from being too smart or too independent. The big push was to get young girls married as soon as possible. In 1951, for example, one-third of all brides were under nineteen years of age.

The industry's problems plus the nation's attitudes affected the screen actress. She found herself in roles designed to show men superior to women. For almost the entire decade, she was preoccupied with the issue of marriage.

Some movies showed how older, unmarried women became mentally ill or pathetic. Bette Davis in *All About Eve* (1950) displayed what happens to an aging star without a husband. Vivien Leigh in *A Streetcar Named Desire* (1951) explored the neuroses of a lonely, unmarried southern belle.

Another group of films showed single women how to catch a husband. Betty Grable, Lauren Bacall, and new star Marilyn Monroe played fortune hunters in *How to Marry a Millionaire* (1953). Dorothy McGuire, Jean Peters, and

Three stunning women plotting together to trap rich husbands formed the story for *How to Marry a Millionaire* (1953). Betty Grable was the wholesome gold digger. Marilyn Monroe was the dumb and sexy blonde who was terrified to wear her eyeglasses in front of a man. Lauren Bacall played the smartest of the three women and ran the show.

All About Eve (1950) gave Bette Davis one of her finest roles. She played the aging Margo Channing, a great star whose life is challenged by the scheming Eve Harrington (played by Anne Baxter, at left). In the end, her director (Gary Merrill, standing) and lifelong friends (Celeste Holm and Hugh Marlowe) help Margo through her problems.

Maggie McNamara found romance overseas in *Three Coins in the Fountain* (1954). Katharine Hepburn suggested spinsters might find success on a Venetian vacation in *Summertime* (1955).

Other movies gave advice to widows. Jennifer Jones enjoyed momentary happiness as a love-struck doctor in Hong Kong during the Korean War in *Love Is a Many Splendored Thing* (1955). Jane Wyman fell in love with a younger man in *All That Heaven Allows* (1955).

For the most part these formula films ignored reality. Women were shown as unfulfilled without a man. Love was better than a career; marriage was better than a romance or divorce. The biggest effect on women in the audience was to make them more conscious of their age and their looks. The cosmetic industry boomed. Beauty salons increased by 30 percent. Manufacturers of padded bras and girdles did a multimillion dollar business. In short, the movies had turned back to the youth cult of the twenties.

A 1953 film changed the pattern. Otto Preminger made a screen version of the popular stage play *The Moon Is Blue*. It was a foolish story about a "virgin" who was being courted by two men. But the powerful Breen Office which administered the Production Code found the film objectionable; the words "virgin" and "seduce" were described as indecent. The issues of adultery and seduction shocked censors across the country. As a result, the picture was refused the Breen Office's Seal of Approval. United Artists, the studio releasing *The Moon Is Blue*, rebelled. It quit the Motion Picture Producers and Distributors Association. The film then went into release and made a big profit. Eventually the Supreme Court defended its right to be shown.

Soon after that case, Joseph Breen retired. He was replaced by Geoffrey Shurlock, an English-born Episcopalian who disliked the Code that had gripped Hollywood since 1933. Determined to free the industry from its "outdated" values, his big chance came in 1956.

Elia Kazan's *Baby Doll* provided the test case for the industry. The story focused on Carroll Baker as the dim-witted child bride of a southern cotton-gin boss. His business rival decides to seduce the sexy wife as a means of destroying the husband. Shurlock gave *Baby Doll* his Seal of Approval. An uproar started. *Time* said *Baby Doll* was ". . . the dirtiest American-made motion picture that has been legally exhibited." Catholic clergy put a six-month boycott on attendance of the film.

But this time the censors met defeat. Hollywood's money troubles made her bolder. The church no longer seemed able to hurt movies at the box office. Controversial films made money. In addition, television, by becoming the mass entertainment form, had given moving pictures more dignity. Movies were now looked upon as ready for serious subjects. Still further, intellectuals argued that neither the church nor any religious group had the right to dictate policy to a private, independent industry. It was an argument that won support from every circle. In the end, even the Legion of Decency bowed to public opinion and revised its criteria for rating films.

Hollywood's portrayal of women changed cautiously during these censorship battles. Yet the difference in attitudes toward marriage was clear. Film makers were more willing

In an attempt to find popular formulas, Hollywood turned to the successful stage plays of Tennessee Williams. *A Streetcar Named Desire* (1951) provided Vivien Leigh with her greatest role, Blanche Du Bois, an aging southern belle whose neurotic fantasies make her unfit for the real world. The performance won the star her second Oscar. Marlon Brando played her savage brother-in-law.

Natalie Wood specialized in the problems adolescent girls were
having in the fifties. She needed to be loved by her parents
and at the same time had to learn to cope with her budding
sexual desires. In *Rebel Without a Cause* (1955) she joined
with James Dean to fight against a world they both resented.

to criticize married life. Grace Kelly faithfully kept her marriage vows, but showed how alcoholic husbands mistreated their wives in *The Country Girl* (1954). Natalie Wood championed the idea that bad marriages wrecked kids' lives in *Rebel Without a Cause* (1955). Elizabeth Taylor revealed how much a wife had to work to make her marriage successful in *Giant* (1956). By 1957, Joanne Woodward could discuss how stupid parents and bad marriages made women neurotic in *The Three Faces of Eve*.

Elizabeth Taylor gave a new look to southern belles in *Giant* (1956). As in most of her mid-fifties roles, Taylor challenged the existing social values about women's place in society. James Dean, another symbolic rebel of the decade, played the misunderstood man next door. He died before the film was released.

Marilyn Monroe was the great sex symbol of the fifties. Yet behind her famous screen image was a sensitive, scared, and helpless woman. Only once during the decade did she have a chance to reveal that true side of herself. The film was *Bus Stop* (1956). Don Murray played the innocent cowboy who discovered that the girl he loved was much more complex than she appeared to be.

The issue of marriage also affected the decade's stars. Three major types surfaced.

One was the sex queen out for a good time and headed for trouble. Marilyn Monroe was unsurpassed in that category. Her beauty was a brilliant product of the Hollywood dream industry. Cameras gazed lovingly at her shapely form. A special lipstick created just for her accented the star's lips. A unique bleaching formula made her hair appear strikingly blonde. Yet Monroe had more than beauty. She made audiences sense that underneath the glitter she was an unstable, unhappy, and unsatisfied woman. In that sense, Monroe bore a strong resemblance to Harlow. Throughout the fifties, she sang and danced and laughed in one film after another, each one covering up the real woman. Only as Cherie, the sexy entertainer in *Bus Stop* (1956), did the real Monroe come through. She taught men to respect her for what she was and not for how she looked.

The second group of stars during the fifties symbolized the-girl-next-door. The queen of the category, Doris Day, played the opposite of the Monroe character. She never made herself over to win a man's heart. In fact, to hide her big bust, Day wore oversized suits, shirts, and dresses to appear small and wholesome. Her roles reminded old-timers of the child-women played by Mary Pickford and Lillian Gish. Day was pure, natural, and sexless. Her most popular films, like *Pillow Talk* (1959), stressed an innocent war between the sexes. Men desired her because she was spunky, beautiful, and played hard to get.

Yet there was something about the Doris Day character that audiences are only now beginning to discover. She made a strong case for career women. Her roles often suggested that females had more than good looks and domestic talents. As film critic Molly Haskell points out, Day's roles gave her jobs that showed ". . . she worked because she loved it, was good at it, and needed the money; not just to find a husband."

Doris Day presented audiences with an alternative to the Monroe image. Naïve when it came to sex, the popular Day image accented naturalness and good, clean fun. Fans liked her best as the interior decorator who shared a party line with Rock Hudson in *Pillow Talk* (1959). A more thoughtful look at the film reveals she also worked hard to make career women creditable.

The third category was reserved for actresses who could play both sensuous and innocent women. Elizabeth Taylor led the parade. Unlike Monroe and Day, who rarely changed their images, Taylor changed with the times. She had started her career as a young, sweet girl in *National Velvet* (1944) and *A Date with Judy* (1948). When the fifties began, M-G-M turned her into a pure young woman in *Father of the Bride* (1950) and *A Place in the Sun* (1951). By the mid-fifties, she had become the troubled wife in search of love in *Raintree County* (1957) and *Cat on a Hot Tin Roof* (1958).

The brilliance of Elizabeth Taylor was in her acting ability. No matter what role she played, audiences found her appealing. She could be mean but also desirable. Her women could be beautiful and strong or lonely and weak. Like the other legendary Hollywood stars, Elizabeth Taylor grew more impressive with each passing decade.

Even so, the stars, the noncontroversial movies, and the big screens could not make enough money to save the movie industry. By the end of the decade, Hollywood was making most of its money from television, not films. The old guard of censors, producers, and directors had died or left. A new generation of businessmen was facing the problems of rebuilding a once great empire.

By the end of the fifties, Hollywood was still obsessed with marriage and southern women. Elizabeth Taylor reached one of the high points in her long career as the frustrated wife in *Cat on a Hot Tin Roof* (1958). Based on a Tennessee Williams stage play, the story focused on a southern family ruled by a dying father. Burl Ives played the overbearing parent; Paul Newman, his confused son.

CHAPTER 6
CRISIS YEARS

The number of successful film actresses in the sixties did not equal the number of fingers on a single hand.

Money was one reason. It just cost too much to make a lot of movies. Production expenses had risen by more than 50 percent over the past decade; salaries of stars, producers, and directors had also skyrocketed. Movie attendance was a second reason. The sixties witnessed a mass migration out of the cities and into the suburbs. The new suburbanites had different leisure habits. They preferred outdoor activities to indoor movies. In 1960, for example, as compared with 1946, movie attendance dropped by 50 million people per week. The average weekly attendance for the entire decade never went beyond 20 million. Television was a third reason. The public saw old movies every day and night for free on the tube. Unless there was something special about a new picture, few people went to the movie theaters.

Added to these problems were audience tastes. The sixties produced an amazing change in the nation's values and habits. Women, in particular, were on the march against the old standards. Birth-control pills gave women more sexual freedom; the issue of legalized abortion was hotly debated; and the institution of marriage came under attack. A college education became the norm for girls as well as boys. For mothers, careers became more and more common. In short, a sexual revolution was under way.

Always looking for some way to satisfy audience tastes, Hollywood began the sixties by making streetwalkers popular heroines. In fact, 1960 was called "the year of the prostitute." Elizabeth Taylor played an ill-fated call girl hungering for suburbia in *Butterfield 8*. The part won her the Oscar for Best Actress. Shirley Jones in a somewhat similar role copped the Oscar for Best Supporting Actress. Normally cast as the-girl-next-door, Jones appeared as a deacon's daughter who is seduced by a fake preacher and then becomes a hooker in *Elmer Gantry*. Less acclaimed but far more popular was Nancy Kwan's role as an Oriental hustler in *The World of Suzie Wong*.

The modest success of such roles encouraged film makers to be more daring in their treatment of this once-taboo subject. Shirley MacLaine revealed what American businessmen did when they "worked late" at the office in *The Apartment* (1960). MacLaine was the gullible mistress who almost had to kill herself to find true love.

Shirley MacLaine was one of the most original actresses of the sixties. Her specialty was the "friendly Bohemian." Producers cast her as the girl men love to pick up. In *The Apartment* (1960), MacLaine played an elevator operator who became an executive's mistress. Jack Lemmon was the man who changed her life.

Audrey Hepburn, another innocent heroine of the fifties, became the kooky, mod chick who got fifty dollars a date in *Breakfast at Tiffany's* (1961). Like MacLaine, Hepburn in the end switched from bachelor pads to marital love. Piper Laurie, still another girl-next-door type, was not so lucky. In *The Hustler* (1961), she found sex destructive and committed suicide. Each of these movies and others like them reflected the sexual revolution taking place in society. Their purpose was not only to make money but also to break down the puritanical values of the Code.

American film makers also specialized in psychotics, drunks, and abused young girls. Bette Davis and Joan Craw-

Audrey Hepburn symbolized "the free spirit" and enchanted audiences with her youthful innocence. One of her most unusual roles was that of Holly Golightly in *Breakfast at Tiffany's* (1961), a part originally written for Marilyn Monroe. When Monroe backed out, Hepburn agreed to do the film on the condition that Holly's swinging ways would be shown sympathetically. George Peppard played her romantic upstairs friend.

ford horrified their fans in *What Ever Happened to Baby Jane?* (1962). Davis appeared as a psychotic ex-child star who cruelly cared for sister Crawford. Lee Remick became the decade's classic drunk in *Days of Wine and Roses* (1962), and Natalie Wood portrayed young girls tragically falling in love in *West Side Story* (1961) and *Love with the Proper Stranger* (1963).

Typical of the way in which movies were attacking traditional values was Wood's role in *Splendor in the Grass* (1961). She played a young high school girl living in Kansas who falls in love with a fellow student. Terrified by their sexual desires, the two teen-agers are confused about how they are supposed to behave with each other. Their parents are no help; their advice is to control sexual emotions. Such feelings are criticized as evil and unhealthy. As a result, the lovers break up. The girl suffers an emotional breakdown; her boyfriend also falls apart. Years later the two meet and realize that there is no way to recapture a lost love. Audiences got the point that sexual feelings were not something to be ashamed of.

None of these roles did much for the actresses themselves. The stars "existed" from one film to the next. Films were too risky to repeat the same roles often. In the days of the great studios, a MacLaine or Remick could have made half a dozen movies a year. The public would have gotten to know their "image." With the vertical system gone, such an approach to film-making was unthinkable. In fact, even the superstars were no longer a guarantee at the box office.

The classic example was Elizabeth Taylor. In 1959 Twentieth Century-Fox had found itself near collapse. Thinking that big stars, a cast of thousands, and a massive publicity campaign would save the studio, producer Spyros Skouras began work on the ill-fated *Cleopatra*. For four years the project staggered on. More than $40 million was spent. Elizabeth Taylor captured worldwide headlines, first with

Bette Davis found producers avoiding her as the sixties began. Angered, she decided to make a horror film. The movie was *What Ever Happened to Baby Jane?* (1962). Both Davis and Joan Crawford (left) played has-been child stars who torment each other. The film launched a new career for Davis as the monster queen. Below: Lee Remick was usually cast as a pretty, carefree woman until *Days of Wine and Roses* (1962) gave her a rare chance to demonstrate her acting talent. Remick shocked audiences with her portrayal of a young wife whose drinking problems led to shame and humiliation.

her bad health and then with her passionate love affair with co-star Richard Burton. But when the film was released in 1963, it was a disaster at the box office. *Newsweek* summed up the results by commenting, "For love of her, Caesar gave his heart, Antony gave his life, and Twentieth Century-Fox a corporate treasure."

Actresses by the mid-sixties found their futures ruled by agents, not studios. Films were now the results of "package deals." Independent producers came up with an idea for a movie. They contacted agents of stars, directors, and screenwriters. Together they molded a package that could be offered to a studio or bank for financing. Everything depended on that one film's being a "hit."

Movie versions of broadway musicals seemed the best risk. They also were excellent showcases to introduce new stars. Julie Andrews as Maria von Trapp in *The Sound of Music* (1965) helped the film become one of the biggest box-office hits in movie history. But her name alone was not enough to ensure success. Three years later she appeared in *Star!,* a somewhat similar film package using the elements of a Broadway Show, and the picture lost a fortune. Barbra Streisand, that same year, 1968, starred in *Funny Girl* and confirmed that a top Broadway musical with a new popular personality was great for business.

The rise of the art house was another trend affecting actresses. These small movie houses attracted people interested in foreign films and unusual productions. Audiences discovered a new image of women being shaped by such European directors as Michelangelo Antonioni, Federico Fellini, and François Truffaut.

The art houses also made it possible for low-budget films to be made. Small audiences were at least able to cover the expenses of a non-formula movie. *Nothing but a Man* (1964) was such a film. The remarkable story of a black couple fighting for dignity in an Alabama suburb did not appeal to the general public. But selected people through-

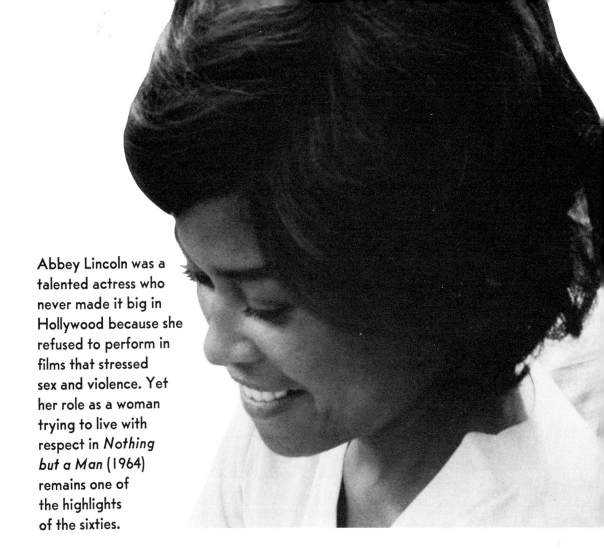

Abbey Lincoln was a talented actress who never made it big in Hollywood because she refused to perform in films that stressed sex and violence. Yet her role as a woman trying to live with respect in *Nothing but a Man* (1964) remains one of the highlights of the sixties.

out the world loved it. They were particularly impressed by actress Abbey Lincoln. Graceful and soft-spoken, she never got a chance for stardom because she was not a "bankable" personality.

Tied to the art-house trend was the move toward international film-making. American producers found it profitable to make movies in different parts of the world. Foreign audiences now made up 50 percent of movie profits. Technicians and production facilities were cheaper outside the United States. International film-making, understandably, increased the importance of European actresses.

Julie Christie was one of the more successful discoveries for American audiences. She had done some minor English movies and gained attention with a small part in the British film *Billy Liar* (1963). Then came her starring role in the international hit *Darling* (1965). The story focused on a modern swinging model who goes from rags to riches. But the Christie character was no Mary Pickford. She was a ruthless woman who found life at the top lonely and bitter. Through her, film makers reflected the manners and mores of the sixties. The message was clear. Enjoy every pleasure you can, because nothing better will come tomorrow.

As the decade wore on, America's establishment values and institutions underwent further attack. The rights of minorities were championed. American participation in the

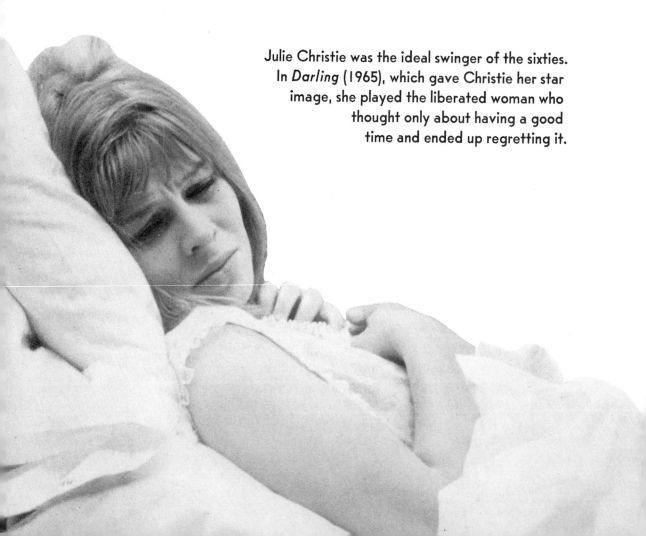

Julie Christie was the ideal swinger of the sixties. In *Darling* (1965), which gave Christie her star image, she played the liberated woman who thought only about having a good time and ended up regretting it.

Vietnam war rocked the faith that many people had in the government. Protests spread across college campuses, arguing that schools should not be involved in war research. Drug use became popular; demonstrations were widespread; violence erupted in the streets; and national figures were assassinated.

Leaders in the movie industry were confused on how to present these issues in the movies. The Motion Picture Code, which had been around since the Depression, was too restricting. Geoffrey Shurlock of the Breen Office had little control over film makers. Eric Johnston, who had replaced Hays in 1945, did not offer much help either. But his sudden death in 1963 left the door open for a new direction. Jack Valenti, ex-political adviser to President Lyndon B. Johnson, became head of the Motion Picture Producers and Distributors Association in 1966. High on his list of priorities was more freedom for the industry. Over the next two years he worked on a new code and, more important, a rating system. Ratings were his idea to help film makers. The ratings would only advise parents as to a movie's suitability for children. The ratings would not judge the quality of a movie. Thus, controversial subjects could be more honestly treated.

On November 1, 1968, the rating game began in the United States. Films were put into four categories. Slightly changed today, the categories are G (general audiences; all ages admitted); PG (parental guidance advised); R (restricted; no one under seventeen admitted without an adult); and X (no one under eighteen admitted).

By 1968, however, the ratings were like closing the barn door after the cow had escaped. "Skin flicks" made by European and independent American film makers had flooded the market. Movie houses showing exclusively "dirty films" were doing big business. Drive-ins, as well, were catering to audiences interested in seeing naked women having sexual romps.

Serious film makers, however, turned their attention to a

new audience of young people between fifteen and thirty years of age. Industry research had discovered that children of the post-World War II era loved movies. They studied them, made them, and spent countless hours watching them. American film makers decided, therefore, that movies would now become "relevant."

From the mid-sixties on, relevance often meant sex, race relations, and gore. Elizabeth Taylor vulgarized herself brilliantly as the shrewish wife in *Who's Afraid of Virginia Woolf?* (1966). Katharine Hepburn was the forward-looking parent who accepted interracial marriage in *Guess Who's Coming to Dinner*. Anne Bancroft became the accepted image of a filthy-rich wife and mother in *The Graduate*. Faye Dunaway mixed sex and violence as the romanticized gun moll in *Bonnie and Clyde* (all in 1967). Joanne Woodward signaled a new look for spinster schoolmarms who no longer let old values rule their lives in *Rachel, Rachel* (1968). Natalie Wood and Dyan Cannon switched husbands in *Bob & Carol & Ted & Alice* (1969) to comment on how new social values were affecting some married couples.

Yet all the "relevant" movies did not put the film industry back on top by the end of the sixties. New leisure habits, few "bankable" stars, costly film failures, and a host of other reasons left most of the major studios weak and helpless. Many were taken over by conglomerates.

The once-famous screen actresses were in even more trouble. They were finding it difficult to get featured roles. A new trend had started. Movies like *The Professionals* (1966), *The Dirty Dozen* and *Cool Hand Luke* (both in 1967), and *Easy Rider* and *Midnight Cowboy* (both in 1969) ignored women and stressed male friendships. Unless they were willing to play girl friends or fallen women, actresses were out of work. Katharine Ross in *Butch Cassidy and the Sundance Kid* (1969) summed up the fears of women approaching thirty, "I'm twenty-six, single, and a schoolteacher. That's the bottom of the pit."

Guess Who's Coming to Dinner (1967) marked Katharine Hepburn's return to movies after a five-year absence. She had spent the time caring for the critically ill Spencer Tracy. To be by Tracy in his last film, she agreed to play the liberal parent who now had to test the truth of her values. Another reason for accepting the role was Hepburn's desire to help her niece Katharine Houghton have a successful debut. Sidney Poitier was the man Houghton wanted to marry.

Who's Afraid of Virginia Woolf? (1966) signaled a new era for Hollywood. Its blunt, blasphemous dialogue gave movies the most shocking language in the history of films. Throwing off her beauty queen image, Elizabeth Taylor played a sloppy, foulmouthed shrew. The performance won her a second Oscar. Richard Burton played the role of her husband.

Joanne Woodward was too old to be a sex symbol and too young to play senior roles. Instead, she chose good character parts. Under husband Paul Newman's direction, she gave meaning to an old-maid schoolteacher's first taste of love in Rachel, Rachel (1968).

Butch Cassidy and the Sundance Kid (1969) was typical of the "buddy" trend in movies. It suggested that men would rather spend time together than in mixed company. Women only became necessary for sex and light companionship. Katharine Ross was the woman who felt that male domination was the only thing left for a spinster schoolmarm over twenty-five. Paul Newman was Butch Cassidy.

CHAPTER 7
NOW AND AFTER

The seventies began with the great Hollywood empire in ruins. Its big studios looked like ghost towns. Sound stages, which once housed fabulous sets, were either quiet "backlots" or property to be sold for high real-estate profits; the fabled legions of stars, directors, producers, screenwriters, and technicians had shrunk to a speck of their former number. But out of the rubble a new Hollywood was taking shape.

Studio organizations became the bankrollers and distributors of movies made by independent film makers. But these new producers and directors, who accounted for 75 percent of American movies, rejected studio facilities. They did their filming, instead, on actual locations throughout the world.

Many forces shaped the way women were portrayed on the screen. High on the list was the status of women in society. They now made up 51.3 percent of the country's population. In actual figures, there were 5.6 million more women than men. A growing number of women were single, divorced, or widowed. Their presence in the work force had nearly doubled since 1950, while that of men had increased by 25 percent. Close to half of the nation's wives and mothers were finding jobs and careers outside the home. The simple fact was that women were more independent than ever before.

Yet independence did not bring equality. Nowhere was this clearer than in the incomes for men and women. In 1974, for example, women's earnings averaged $6,772 compared to $11,835 for men. It was also clear that the blurring of sex roles in business, sports, and the home did not give more power to women. Men still made the major policy decisions.

Film makers discovered that audiences were divided in their feelings about the social revolution. Some felt good that more women could be independent of their husbands. Others worried what would happen to children as parents became more interested in doing "their own thing." Everyone talked about the declining birthrate, divorces, and separations. People wondered how men were supposed to act in a unisex world.

The first films of the decade set off two major trends. One, the "protest" film, was initiated by *Diary of a Mad Housewife* (1970). Carrie Snodgress was the henpecked wife who tries and fails to find self-fulfillment. Her only importance to her husband is as a cook, nurse, sex object, and child rearer. He refuses to treat her as a human being with feelings. Her bratty children are even more abusive. They relate to her only in terms of "Get me this" or "I want that." The idea of the oppressed housewife continued in movies like *Pete 'n' Tillie* (1972) and *Alice Doesn't Live Here Anymore* and *A Woman under the Influence* (both in 1974). By 1975, the idea of the independent housewife became a grisly joke in *The Stepford Wives*, a screenplay that focused on wealthy husbands in Stepford, Connecticut, who kill their outspoken wives and replace them with beautiful, doll-like robots.

Years ago glamourous actresses would have played these roles. Now the emphasis had shifted to dramatic skill. Carrie Snodgress, Ellen Burstyn, and Gena Rowlands showed acting ability, more than beauty or perfect bodies. They seemed real, human, and affected by life around them. Their roles reminded the public that women were entitled to a better life.

But the "protest" films did not do well at the box

office. The public had enough to think about with the Vietnam war, a worldwide food shortage, the threat of nuclear destruction, and pollution of the environment. Once more audiences turned to the movies for escape from their everyday problems.

Love Story (1970) was the film that launched the "entertainment" trend. The plot reworked Hollywood's old tearjerker formula. A boy and girl meet. They fall in love and marry. Tragedy strikes and the girl dies in her husband's arms. Ali MacGraw as the doomed sweetheart made a hit with the public. She was the-girl-next-door given a modern life-style. People left their TV sets by the millions to see the movie. During its opening week, *Love Story* broke box-office records in 159 of the 165 theaters showing the film.

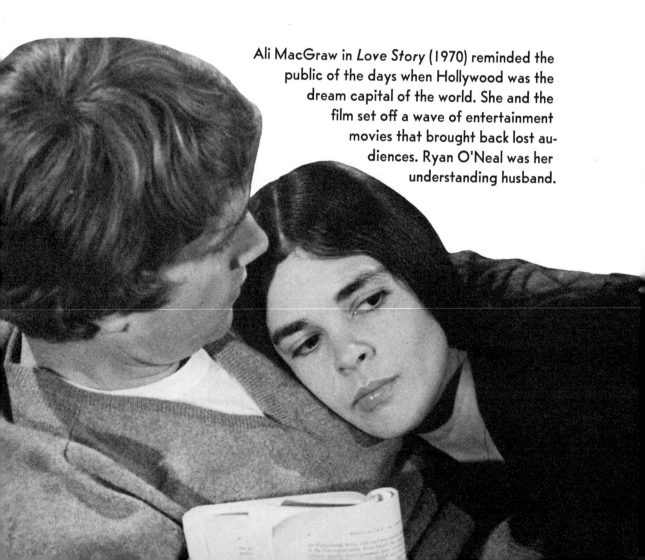

Ali MacGraw in *Love Story* (1970) reminded the public of the days when Hollywood was the dream capital of the world. She and the film set off a wave of entertainment movies that brought back lost audiences. Ryan O'Neal was her understanding husband.

Glenda Jackson is a European woman who prides herself on acting, not beauty. She has worked on the stage, in television, and on the silver screen. For her touching role as a liberated divorcée in *A Touch of Class* (1973), she was awarded the year's Oscar for Best Actress.

Producers got the message. The big money was to be made in avoiding serious themes. What the public really wanted was entertainment: crime stories, musicals, westerns, horror films, women's movies. All that was needed were a few modern touches in dialogue, sex, and gore.

The switch to entertainment gave film actresses a chance to humanize familiar roles. Jane Fonda modernized the big-city call girl trying to reform in *Klute* (1971), a detective film. Westerns allowed Julie Christie to examine the pathetic life of a dope-smoking frontier madam in *McCabe and Mrs. Miller* (1971). Musicals exposed Liza Minnelli to a young singer's bad breaks in *Cabaret* (1972). Horror films made Linda Blair a girl possessed by the devil in *The Exorcist* (1973). Romance movies hit a new high when bright woman Barbra Streisand won pretty man Robert Redford in *The Way We Were* (1973). And comedies made it possible for Glenda Jackson to show the sympathetic side of adultery in *A Touch of Class* (1974).

Liza Minnelli finally overcame the great shadow of her mother, Judy Garland, in *Cabaret* (1972). As Sally Bowles, who wanted to enjoy life at any price, she revealed a personality that audiences appreciated.

Barbra Streisand gave women one of the decade's great fantasies in *The Way We Were* (1973). She played career woman Katie Morosky, who marries her college crush, Robert Redford. What was so unusual about the film was that Redford, not Streisand, became the sex object.

Jane Fonda, one of Hollywood's most independent actresses, gave a stunning performance in *Klute* (1971) as the neurotic call girl who received help from detective Donald Sutherland. After her Oscar-winning performance, she had the power to refuse to appear in any movie she did not believe in.

The switch to entertainment movies affected the Hollywood women in other ways. One area dealt with black actresses. They were used to offset the bad images that many violent movies created about Afro-Americans. Cecily Tyson, who refused to play promiscuous women or maids, hit the jackpot in *Sounder* (1972). Thanks to her stunning role as Rebecca, a hardworking mother and wife, she broke down the racial barriers against black actresses. So did Diana Ross in the Billie Holiday biography, *Lady Sings the Blues* (1972). Two years later Diahann Carroll proved that black women could also make people laugh in the social comedy *Claudine*.

Diahann Carroll starred in one of 1974's best comedies, *Claudine*. The film proved that black and white audiences could sympathize with the problems of a Harlem welfare mother. The role won Carroll an Oscar nomination. James Earl Jones was her new husband.

Cecily Tyson's role of Rebecca in *Sounder* (1972) changed
the image that many Americans had of black women.
Earlier they identified with Louise Beavers in *Imitation of
Life* (1934) and Ethel Waters in *Pinky* (1949). Now they
looked at a woman who was tough, hardworking, lovely, and
very human. Paul Winfield (left) played her husband. Taj
Mahal (right) was the strumming neighbor. Tyson won
an Oscar nomination for Best Actress for her 1972 role.

Diana Ross also broke down racial barriers with her
debut as the legendary Billie Holiday in *Lady Sings
the Blues* (1972). Beautiful and talented, she sang and
laughed to the ways of Richard Pryor in the screen
story of the late blues singer. Ross won an Oscar
nomination for the year's outstanding actress.

A second area affected by the stress on entertainment was the sex film. The seventies had made hard-core sex movies popular. For example, two of the biggest box-office hits were *Deep Throat* (1972) and *The Devil in Miss Jones* (1973). Famous people once frightened to be seen viewing this type of film now went openly. Such "boldness" again gave rise to demands that the movie industry be cleaned up. But this time, a Supreme Court decision in June 1973 put the responsibility in the hands of the average person in local communities. The idea that X-rated movies now needed the approval of every local area terrified many film makers. They began putting their money in R or PG movies. As a result, the need for actresses to undress in front of the cameras became less and less necessary.

But the greatest effect of the entertainment boom was that it gave women fewer big parts. Starting with *The Poseidon Adventure* (1972), film makers turned to "block-buster" movies. The emphasis was on special effects, violence, and male stars. Among the more successful movies were *The Godfather*, Part I (1972), *The Godfather, Part II, Murder on the Orient Express, The Towering Inferno*, and *Earthquake* (all in 1974).

Along with these spectacular movies came a continued interest in "buddy" films. The public paid big money to see movies about male friendships. Heading the list were *M*A*S*H* (1970), *Carnal Knowledge* (1971), *Mean Streets, Papillion, The Sting* (all in 1973), and *The Longest Yard* (1974). The best that actresses could do in such films was to take a small character role.

Thus, we come to the crisis of the seventies—faced by women in American movies. The statistics tell a sad story. *Newsweek* reported in 1974 that the Producers' Guild had 3,060 men and 8 women; the Directors' Guild, 2,343 men and 23 women; the Writers' Guild, 2,828 men and 148 women. In 1975, 72 percent of all speaking roles in American movies went to men. A comparison between the ten biggest money-makers of 1934 and 1974 highlights the issue. Of the top ten box-office stars in 1934, six were women: Janet Gaynor, Joan Crawford, Mae West, Marie Dressler, Norma Shearer, and Shirley Temple. Of the top ten in 1974, only one was a woman: Barbra Streisand.

How have the actresses of the seventies reacted to their second-rate status in the industry?

Some have turned to work outside the movies while they wait for the "right" film. The very best jobs are those found in television. The opportunities are varied.

First, there are the "special" shows. An actress contracts to do a single performance, which not only gives her wide exposure but also keeps her free to do other jobs. Cecily Tyson, for example, drew rave notices for her

Cecily Tyson was another actress who refused to work in just any film. Not until two years after *Sounder* did fans see her in a movie. This time she starred as a fictional 110-year-old former slave who recounts her life of struggle from Civil War days to the civil rights era. For her television role in *The Autobiography of Miss Jane Pittman*, Tyson won an Emmy award.

Cloris Leachman has been a professional actress for more than forty years. Thanks to her work on *The Mary Tyler Moore Show*, the actress was given her own television series, *Phyllis*. In this episode, Phyllis patches up her differences with Judith Lowry (playing the role of Mother Dexter).

Emmy-winning special, *The Autobiography of Miss Jane Pittman* (1974). Jane Alexander scored a hit as the wife of a President in *Eleanor and Franklin* (1976). Lee Remick successfully dramatized the life of Lady Randolph Churchill in a unique seven-part special entitled *Jennie* (also in 1976).

Secondly, television has provided some actresses with a chance for long-term jobs in the form of a series. The advantages to such an arrangement are many. There is a chance to perfect one's techniques, gain much needed experience, and establish an audience identity. A television series, in one sense, does for a performer what the old studio system did for its contract players. Among the actresses benefiting from such an arrangement are Cloris Leachman in *Phyllis;* Angie Dickinson, *Police Woman;* Valerie Harper, *Rhoda;* and Bernadette Peters, *All's Fair.*

Such series do more than make household words of their stars. They show viewers how single and divorced women operate in today's society. Between laughs, the actresses educate a mass audience to new ideas about the modern woman. No longer is she fit only for housecleaning and child rearing. The characters on these series hold responsible jobs and pursue the same goals as their male counterparts. Love and security are put in a new light. They become part of a world that does not necessarily include marriage.

Lindsay Wagner is one such series heroine who is using television as a stepping-stone to the movies. In 1971 she was signed to a film contract by Universal studios. Hoping to get some movie parts, Wagner found herself working mostly in Universal's TV shows. Not even a starring role in the significant movie *The Paper Chase* (1974) made a difference to her bosses. By 1975 she found herself out of work altogether. Then a lucky break in a two-part love

Lindsay Wagner is the star of the American TV series *The Bionic Woman.* For years ignored by film producers, she intends to use her undercover roles on the TV series as rehearsals for major film assignments.

episode on *Six Million Dollar Man* eventually brought Wagner her own TV series, *The Bionic Woman*. But the key to her acceptance of the long-term contract was a clause that promised she would make one-movie-a-year. "No woman ever has progressed," Wagner points out, "from series to film. *Men* have—James Garner, Steve McQueen, George C. Scott—but there have been no leading ladies in television dramatic series." She intends to change that. By playing different types of women in her undercover roles as the bionic woman, Wagner is readying herself for any big movie role that comes along.

A third value of television for film actresses is that it can spoof the traditions of women's movies and soap operas. The best example is the revolutionary series, *Mary Hartman, Mary Hartman*. Its heroine, played superbly by Louise Lasser, is a confused, nervous housewife living in the fictional working-class town of Fernwood, Ohio. Mary's average day finds her in conflict with an impotent husband, a sex-crazy younger sister in love with a lustful policeman, a teen-age daughter who wants to quite school and join an all-girl rock band, and a senile grandfather. Some of the show's favorite topics played for laughs are mass murder, exhibitionism, and venereal disease. Critics are discovering however, that the series is providing mass audiences with a daring and meaningful look at modern society.

Television, however, is not the only way to solve the present crisis of women in film. Another way is to become more involved in the movie business itself. Eleanor Perry is one example. The screenwriter of such films as *David and Lisa* (1962), *Diary of a Mad Housewife* (1970), and *The Man Who Loved Cat Dancing* (1973), Perry has turned to producing movies. Jay Presson Allen is another screenwriter who feels that women themselves must help create better roles for actresses. Among her credits are *The Prime of Miss Jean Brodie* (1969), *Cabaret* (1972), and *Funny Lady* (1975).

Louise Lasser proved to be the ideal heroine for *Mary Hartman, Mary Hartman* on American television. Although Lasser gained some minor fame for her movie roles in *Bananas* (1971) and *Slither* (1973), her career hit a stalemate until the Mary Hartman role. Now she is a household word. Hopefully, television will give the talented actress a chance for future screen roles.

Some stars have decided to make films. "I don't see any light in the studios themselves," complains Shirley MacLaine. "How can they make movies about us when they're not like us? We have to do it. That's why I'm doing it." Her initial project is about the life of the first woman to fly solo around the world, Amelia Earhart. Ellen Burstyn is another star going into the business end of film-making. Her first attempt was *Alice Doesn't Live Here Anymore* (1974). From there she has gone on to a project about a mother alone with her three children in British Columbia during the Depression. While Burstyn finds the film business tough on women, she points out, "It's a time of change and we all have to be educated in the process."

Signs of a change are already apparent in 1976. Key film makers, rebelling against high salary demands by male actors, are casting women in roles originally intended for men. Director John Boorman is a good example. In his upcoming movie *The Heretic—Exorcist II,* he originally wanted a male star to portray a New York City psychiatrist. When he found that big name actors were too expensive for his budget, he decided to make the doctor a woman and assigned the part to Louise Fletcher. Other film makers are now following this new trend.

Another encouraging sign is the success of the Second International Festival of Women's Films held in New York City during September 1976. Started four years before by Kristina Nordstrom and Leah Laiman, the festival has become a showcase for revivals of important features and shorts by women directors, panel discussions on the problems faced by women in the media, and exposure for recent, overlooked films such as Margarethe von Trotta's *The Lost Honor of Katharine Blum* starring Jeanne Moreau.

What the future holds for the Hollywood woman is uncertain. But we do know that her image and roles depend upon more than the whims of a male-dominated industry. They rely on audience tastes, on economic conditions, on the goals of the film makers themselves, on pressures outside the industry, and on the close links between movies and society. More women in the business end of film-making is not the whole answer, but to do anything without women is unthinkable. Jane Fonda may have said it best: "I think the only way to survive as an artist is to be in step with history, to be plugged into *life* and to be always open to changing and growing and being courageous and not just looking out for your own skin."

BIBLIOGRAPHY

The author hopes that the following selective reading list which he used in writing this book will help the interested person to explore more fully the history of women in American films.

"Ali MacGraw: A Return to Basics," *Time* 97 (January 11, 1971), pp. 40–45.

Brown, Curtis F. *Ingrid Bergman*. New York: Pyramid Publications, 1973.

"Cinema," *Time* 68 (December 24, 1956), p. 61.

"Cloris," *TV Guide* (October 25, 1975), pp. 6–10.

Corliss, Richard. *Greta Garbo*. New York: Pyramid Publications, 1974.

Davidson, Bill. "The 'Bionic Woman' Flexed Her Financial Muscles . . .," *TV Guide* (May 8, 1975), pp. 21–26.

Davies, Marion. *The Times We Had: Life with William Randolph Hearst*. New York: Bobbs-Merrill, 1975.

Diehl, Digby. "Police Woman," *TV Guide* (January 4, 1975), pp. 22–25.

Gish, Lillian. *The Movies, Mr. Griffith, and Me*. Englewood Cliffs, N.J.: Prentice-Hall, 1969.

Harvey, Stephen. *Joan Crawford*. New York: Pyramid Publications, 1974.

Haskell, Molly. *From Reverence to Rape: The Treatment of Women in the Movies*. New York: Holt, Rinehart and Winston, 1974.

———. "Doris Day's Films: Against and Ahead of Her Time," *Ms.* 4 (January 1976), pp. 56–57.

Higham, Charles. *Hollywood at Sunset*. New York: Saturday Review Press, 1972.

Hirsch, Foster. *Elizabeth Taylor*. New York: Pyramid Publications, 1973.

Israel, Lee. "Women in Film: Saving an Endangered Species," *Ms.* 3 (February 1975), pp. 51–57, 104.

Jowett, Garth. *Film: The Democratic Art*. Boston: Little Brown, 1976.

Juneau, James. *Judy Garland*. New York: Pyramid Publications, 1974.

Klemesrud, Judy. "Do Any of These Actresses Rate an Academy Award?" *The New York Times* II (February 8, 1976), pp. 1, 19.

"Liberated Women: How They're Changing American Life—Interviews with 2 Experts," *U.S. News & World Report* 80 (June 7, 1976), pp. 46–49.

Manchel, Frank. *The Talking Clowns: From Laurel and Hardy to the Marx Brothers*. New York: Franklin Watts, 1976.

Manvell, Roger. *Love Goddesses of the Movies*. New York: Paul Hamlyn Books, 1975.

Marill, Alvin H. *Katharine Hepburn*. New York: Pyramid Publications, 1973.

Mellen, Joan. *Marilyn Monroe*. New York: Pyramid Publications, 1973.

Merritt, Russell, "Nickelodeon Theaters," *AFI Report* 4:2 (May 1973), pp. 4–8.

Mohanna, Christine. "A One-Sided Story: Women in the Movies," *Women and Film* I (1972), pp. 7–12.

Moore, Colleen. *Silent Star*. New York: Doubleday, 1968.

Negri, Pola. *Memoirs of a Star*. New York: Doubleday, 1970.

"The New Movies." *Newsweek* (December 7, 1972), pp. 62–74.

O'Hallaren, Bill. "A Cute Tomato, A Couple of Slices of Baloney, Some Sour Grapes, A Few Nuts . . . ," *TV Guide* (June 19, 1976), pp. 16–19.

Quigley, Martin, Jr., and Richard Gertner. *Films in America: 1929–1969*. New York: Golden Press, 1970.

Rosen, Marjorie. *Popcorn Venus: Women, Movies & the American Dream*. New York: Coward, McCann & Geoghegan, 1973.

Sklar, Robert. *Movie-Made America: A Social History of Movies*. New York: Random House, 1975.

Slide, Anthony. *The Griffith Actresses*. Cranbury, N.J.: A. S. Barnes, 1973.

Spada, James. *Barbra—The First Decade: The Films and Career of Barbra Streisand*. Secaucus, N.J.: Citadel Press, 1975.

Stern, Lee Edward. *The Movie Musical*. New York: Pyramid Publications, 1974.

Vermilye, Jerry. *Barbara Stanwyck*. New York: Pyramid Publications, 1975.

———. *Bette Davis*. New York: Pyramid Publications, 1973.

Waters, Harry F., with Martin Kasindorf. "The Mary Hartman Craze," *Newsweek* (May 3, 1976), pp. 54–56, 61, 63.

Weltman, Manuel, and Raymond Lee. *Pearl White, The Peerless Fearless Girl*. Cranbury, N.J.: A. S. Barnes, 1970.

Wilson, John M. "Jane Fonda's Happy Heist," *The New York Times* II (April 11, 1976), p. 1.

Windeler, Robert. *Sweetheart: The Story of Mary Pickford*. New York: Praeger, 1973.

INDEX